Historic Doubts on the Life and Reign

of King Richard the Third

by

by Horace Walpole

First Published 1768.

L'histoire n'est fondee que sur le tomoignage des Auteurs qui nous l'ont transmisse. Il importe donc extremement, pour la scavoir, de bien connoitre quels etoient ces Auteurs. Rien n'est a negliger en ce point; le tems ou ils ont vecu, leur naissance, leur patrie, le part qu'ils ont eue aux affaires, les moyens par lesquels ils ont ete instruits, et l'interet qu'ils y pouvaient prendre, sont des circonstances essentielles qu'il n'est pas permis d'ignorer: dela depend le plus ou le moins d'autorite qu'ils doivent avoir: et sans cette connoissance, on courra risque tres souvent de prendre pour guide un Historien de mauvaisse foi, ou du moins, mal informe. Hist. de l'Acad. des Inscript. Vol. X.

LONDON

PREFACE

So incompetent has the generality of historians been for the province they have undertaken, that it is almost a question, whether, if the dead of past ages could revive, they would be able to reconnoitre the events of their own times, as transmitted to us by ignorance and misrepresentation. All very ancient history, except that of the illuminated Jews, is a perfect fable. It was written by priests, or collected from their reports; and calculated solely to raise lofty ideas of the origin of each nation. Gods and demi-gods were the principal actors; and truth is seldom to be expected where the personages are supernatural. The Greek historians have no advantage over the Peruvian, but in the beauty of their language, or from that language being more familiar to us. Mango Capac, the son of the sun, is as authentic a founder of a royal race, as the progenitor of the Heraclidae. What truth indeed could be expected, when even the identity of person is uncertain? The actions of one were ascribed to many, and of many to one. It is not known whether there was a single Hercules or twenty.

As nations grew polished. History became better authenticated. Greece itself learned to speak a little truth. Rome, at the hour of its fall, had the consolation of seeing the crimes of its usurpers published. The vanquished inflicted eternal wounds on their conquerors—but who knows, if Pompey had succeeded, whether Julius Caesar would not have been decorated as a martyr to publick liberty? At some periods the suffering criminal captivates all hearts; at others, the triumphant tyrant. Augustus, drenched in the blood of his fellow-citizens, and Charles Stuart, falling in his own blood, are held up to admiration.

Truth is left out of the discussion; and odes and anniversary sermons give the law to history and credulity.

But if the crimes of Rome are authenticated, the case is not the same with its virtues. An able critic has shown that nothing is more problematic than the history of the three or four first ages of that city. As the confusions of the state increased, so do the confusions in its story. The empire had masters, whose names are only known from medals. It is uncertain of what princes several empresses were the wives. If the jealousy of two antiquaries intervenes, the point becomes inexplicable. Oriuna, on the medals of Carausius, used to pass for the moon: of late years it is become a doubt whether she was not his consort. It is of little importance whether she was moon or empress: but 'how little must we know of those times, when those land-marks to certainty, royal names, do not serve even that purpose! In the cabinet of the king of France are several coins of sovereigns, whose country cannot now be guessed at.

The want of records, of letters, of printing, of critics; wars, revolutions, factions, and other causes, occasioned these defects in ancient history. Chronology and astronomy are forced to tinker up and reconcile, as well as they can, those uncertainties. This satisfies the learned—but what should we think of the reign of George thc Second, to be calculated two thousand years hence by eclipses, lest the conquest of Canada should be ascribed to James the First.

At the very moment that the Roman empire was resettled, nay, when a new metropolis was erected, in an age of science and arts, while letters still held up their heads in Greece; consequently, when the great outlines of truth, I mean events, might be expected to be established; at that very period a new deluge of error burst upon the world. Cristian monks and saints laid truth waste; and a mock sun rose at Rome, when the Roman sun sunk at Constantinople. Virtues and vices were rated by the standard of bigotry; and the militia of the church became the only historians. The best princes were represented as monsters; the worst, at least the most useless, were deified, according as they depressed or exalted turbulent and enthusiastic prelates and friars. Nay, these men were so destitute of temper and common sense, that they dared to suppose that common sense would never revisit the earth: and accordingly wrote with so little judgment, and committed such palpable forgeries, that if we cannot discover what really happened in those ages, we can at least he very sure what did not. How many general persecutions does the church record, of which there is not the smallest trace? What donations and charters were forged, for which those holy persons would lose their ears, if they were in this age to present them in the most common court of judicature? Yet how long were these impostors the only persons who attempted to write history!

But let us lay aside their interested lies, and consider how far they were qualified in other respects to transmit faithful memoirs to posterity. In the ages I speak of, the barbarous monkish ages, the shadow of learning that existed was confined to the clergy: they generally wrote in Latin, or in verse, and their compositions in both were truly barbarous. The difficulties of rhime, and the want of correspondent terms in Latin, were no small impediments to the severe nvarch of truth. But there were worse obstacles to encounter. Europe was in a continual state of warfare. Little princes and great lords were constantly skirmishing and struggling for trifling additions of territory, or wasting each others borders. Geography was very imperfect; no police existed; roads, such as they were, were dangerous; and posts were not established. Events were only known by rumour, from pilgrims, or by letters carried In couriers to the parties interested: the public did not enjoy even those fallible vehicles of intelligence, newspapers. In this situation did monks, at twenty, fifty, an hundred, nay, a thousand miles distance (and under the circumstances I have mentioned even twenty miles were considerable) undertake to write history—and they wrote it accordingly.

If we take a survey of our own history, and examine it with any attention, what an unsatisfactory picture does it present to us! How dry, how superficial, how void of information! How little is recorded besides battles, plagues, and religious foundations! That this should be the case, before the Conquest, is not surprizing. Our empire was but forming itself, or re-collecting its divided members into one mass, which, from the desertion of the Romans, had split into petty kingdoms. The invasions of nations as barbarous as ourselves, interfered with every plan of policy and order that might have been formed to settle the emerging state; and swarms of foreign monks were turned loose upon us with their new faith and mysteries, to bewilder and confound the plain good sense of our ancestors. It was too much to have Danes, Saxons, and Popes, to combat at once! Our language suffered as much as our government; and not having acquired much from our Roman masters, was miserably disfigured by the subsequent invaders. The unconquered parts of the island retained some purity and some precision. The Welsh and Erse tongues wanted not harmony: but never did exist a more barbarous jargon than the dialect, still venerated by antiquaries, and called Saxon. It was so uncouth, so inflexible to all composition, that the monks, retaining the idiom, were reduced to write in what they took or meant for Latin.

The Norman tyranny succeeded, and gave this Babel of savage sounds a wrench towards their own language. Such a mixture necessarily required ages to bring it to some standard: and, consequently, whatever compositions were formed during its progress, were sure of growing obsolete. However, the authors of those days were not likely to make these obvious reflections; and indeed seem to have aimed at no one perfection. From the Conquest to the reign of Henry the Eighth it is difficult to discover any one beauty in our writers, but their simplicity. They told their tale, like story-tellers; that is, they related without art or ornament; and they related whatever they heard. No councils of princes, no motives of conduct, no remoter springs of action, did they investigate or learn. We have even little light into the characters of the actors. A king or an archbishop of Canterbury are the only persons with whom we are made much acquainted. The barons are all represented as brave patriots; but we have not the satisfaction of knowing which, of them were really so; nor whether they were not all turbulent and ambitious. The probability is, that both kings and nobles wished to encroach on each other, and if any sparks of liberty were struck out in all likelihood it was contrary to the intention of either the flint or the steel.

Hence it has been thought necessary to give a new dress to English history. Recourse has been had to records, and they are far from corroborating the testimonies of our historians. Want of authentic memorials has obliged our later writers to leave the mass pretty much as they found it. Perhaps all the requisite attention that might have been bestowed, has not been bestowed. It demands great industry and patience to wade into such abstruse stores as records and charters: and they being jejune and narrow in themselves, very acute criticism is necessary to strike light from their assistance. If they solemnly contradict historians in material facts, we may lose our history; but it is impossible to adhere to our historians. Partiality man cannot intirely divest himself of; it is so natural, that the bent of a writer to one side or the other of a question is almost always discoverable. But there is a wide difference between favouring and lying and yet I doubt whether the whole stream of our historians, misled by their originals, have not falsified one reign in our annals in the grossest manner. The moderns are only guilty of taking-on trust what they ought to have examined more scrupulously, as the authors whom they copied were all ranked on one side in a flagrant season of party. But no excuse can be made for the original authors, who, I doubt, have violated all rules of truth.

The confusions which attended the civil war between the houses of York and Lancaster, threw an obscurity over that part of our annals, which it is almost impossible to dispel. We have scarce any authentic monuments of the reign of Edward the Fourth; and ought to read his history with much distrust, from the boundless partiality of the succeeding writers to the opposite cause. That diffidence should increase as we proceed to the reign of his brother.

It occurred to me some years ago, that the picture of Richard the Third, as drawn by historians, was a character formed by prejudice and invention. I did not take Shakespeare's tragedy for a genuine representation, but I did take the story of that reign for a tragedy of imagination. Many of the crimes imputed to Richard seemed improbable; and, what was stronger, contrary to his interest. A few incidental circumstances corroborated my opinion; an original and important instrument was pointed out to me last winter, which gave rise to the following' sheets; and as it was easy to perceive, under all the glare of encomiums which historians have heaped on the wisdom of

Henry the Seventh, that he was a mean and unfeeling tyrant, I suspected that they had blackened his rival, till Henry, by the contrast, should appear in a kind of amiable light. The more I examined their story, the more I was confirmed in my opinion: and with regard to Henry, one consequence I could not help drawing; that we have either no authentic memorials of Richard's crimes, or, at most, no account of them but from Lancastrian historians; whereas the vices and injustice of Henry are, though palliated, avowed by the concurrent testimony of his panegyrists. Suspicions and calumny were fastened on Richard as so many assassinations. The murders committed by Henry were indeed executions and executions pass for prudence with prudent historians; for when a successful king is chief justice, historians become a voluntary jury.

If I do not flatter myself, I have unravelled a considerable part of that dark period. Whether satisfactory or not, my readers must decide. Nor is it of any importance whether I have or not. The attempt was mere matter of curiosity and speculation. If any man, as idle as myself, should take the trouble to review and canvass my arguments I am ready to yield so indifferent a point to better reasons. Should declamation alone be used to contradict me, I shall not think I am less in the right.

Nov. 28th, 1767.

HISTORIC DOUBTS ON THE LIFE AND REIGN OF KING RICHARD III.

There is a kind of literary superstition, which men are apt to contract from habit, and which-makes them look On any attempt towards shaking their belief in any established characters, no matter whether good or bad, as a sort of prophanation. They are determined to adhere to their first impressions, and are equally offended at any innovation, whether the person, whose character is to be raised or depressed, were patriot or tyrant, saint or sinner. No indulgence is granted to those who would ascertain the truth. The more the testimonies on either side have been multiplied, the stronger is the conviction; though it generally happens that the original evidence is wonderous slender, and that the number of writers have but copied one another; or, what is worse, have only added to the original, without any new authority. Attachment so groundless is not to be regarded; and in mere matters of curiosity, it were ridiculous to pay any deference to it. If time brings new materials to light, if facts and dates confute historians, what does it signify that we have been for two or three hundred years under an error? Does antiquity consecrate darkness? Does a lie become venerable from its age?

Historic justice is due to all characters. Who would not vindicate Henry the Eighth or Charles the Second, if found to be falsely traduced? Why then not Richard the Third? Of what importance is it to any man living whether or not he was as bad as he is represented? No one noble family is sprung from him.

However, not to disturb too much the erudition of those who have read the dismal story of his cruelties, and settled their ideas of his tyranny and usurpation, I declare I am not going to write a vindication of him. All I mean to show, is, that though he may have been as execrable as we are told he was, we have little or no reason to believe so. If the propensity of habit should still incline a single man to suppose that all he has read of Richard is true, I beg no more, than that that person would be so impartial as to own that he has little or no foundation for supposing so.

I will state the list of the crimes charged on Richard; I will specify the authorities on which he was accused; I will give a faithful account of the historians by whom he was accused; and will then examine the circumstances of each crime and each evidence; and lastly, show that some of the crimes were contrary to Richard's interest, and almost all inconsistent with probability or with dates, and some of them involved in material contradictions.

Supposed crimes of Richard the Third.

1st. His murder of Edward prince of Wales, son of Henry the Sixth.

2d. His murder of Henry the Sixth.

3d. The murder of his brother George duke of Clarence.

4th. The execution of Rivers, Gray, and Vaughan.

5th, The execution of Lord Hastings.

6th. The murder of Edward the Fifth and his brother.

7th. The murder of his own queen.

To which may be added, as they are thrown into the list to blacken him, his intended match with his own niece Elizabeth, the penance of Jane Shore, and his own personal deformities.

I. Of the murder of Edward prince of Wales, son of Henry the Sixth.

Edward the Fourth had indubitably the hereditary right to the crown; which he pursued with singular bravery and address, and with all the arts of a politician and the cruelty of a conqueror. Indeed on neither side do there seem to have been any scruples: Yorkists and Lancastrians, Edward and Margaret of Anjou, entered into any engagements, took any oaths, violated them, and indulged their revenge, as often as they were depressed or victorious. After the battle of Tewksbury, in which Margaret and her son were made prisoners, young Edward was brought to the presence of Edward the Fourth; "but after the king," says Fabian, the oldest historian of those times, "had questioned with the said Sir Edwarde, and he had answered unto hym contrary his pleasure, he then strake him with his gauntlet upon the face; after which stroke, so by him received, he was by the kynges servants incontinently slaine." The chronicle of Croyland of the same date says, "the prince was slain 'ultricibus quorundam manibus';" but names nobody.

Hall, who closes his word with the reign of Henry the Eighth, says, that "the prince beyinge bold of stomache and of a good courag, answered the king's question (of how he durst so presumptuously enter into his realme with banner displayed) sayinge, to recover my fater's kingdome and enheritage, &c. at which wordes kyng Edward said nothing, but with his hand thrust him from him, or, as some say, stroke him with his gauntlet, whome incontinent, they that stode about, which were George duke of Clarence, Richard duke of Gloucester, Thomas marques Dorset (son of queen Elizabeth Widville) and William lord Hastinges, sodainly murthered and pitiously manquelled." Thus much had the story gained from the time of Fabian to that of Hall.

Hollingshed repeats these very words, consequently is a transcriber, and no new authority.

John Stowe reverts to Fabian's account, as the only one not grounded on hear-say, and affirms no more, than that the king cruelly smote the young prince on the face with his gauntlet, and after his servants slew him.

Of modern historians, Rapin and Carte, the only two who seem not to have swallowed implicitly all the vulgar tales propagated by the Lancastrians to blacken the house of York, warn us to read with allowance the exaggerated relations of those times. The latter suspects, that at the dissolution of the monasteries all evidences were suppressed that tended to weaken the right of the prince on the throne; but as Henry the Eighth concentred in himself both the claim of Edward the Fourth and that ridiculous one of Henry the Seventh, he seems to have had less occasion to be anxious lest the truth should come out; and indeed his father had involved that truth in so much darkness, that it was little likely to force its way. Nor was it necessary then to load the memory of Richard the Third, who had left no offspring. Henry the Eighth had no competitor to fear but the descendants of Clarence, of whom he seems to have had sufficient apprehension, as appeared by his murder of the old countess of Salisbury, daughter of Clarence, and his endeavours to root out her posterity. This jealousy accounts for Hall charging the duke of Clarence, as well as the duke of Gloucester, with the murder of prince Edward. But in accusations of so deep a dye, it is not sufficient ground for our belief, that an historian reports them with such a frivolous palliative as that phrase, "as some say". A cotemporary names the king's servants as perpetrators of the murder: Is not that more probable, than that the king's own brothers should have dipped their hands in so foul an assassination? Richard, in particular, is allowed on all hands to have been a brave and martial prince: he had great share in the victory at Tewksbury: Some years afterwards, he commanded his brother's troops in Scotland, and made himself master of Edinburgh. At the battle of Bosworth, where he fell, his courage was heroic: he sought Richmond, and endeavoured to decide their quarrel by a personal combat, slaying Sir William Brandon, his rival's standard-bearer, with his own hand, and felling to the ground Sir John Cheney, who endeavoured to oppose his fury. Such men may be carried by ambition to command the execution of those who stand in their way; but are not likely to lend their hand, in cold blood, to a base, and, to themselves, useless assassination. How did it import Richard in what manner the young prince was put to death? If he had so early planned the ambitious designs ascribed to him, he might have trusted to his brother Edward, so much more immediately concerned, that the young prince would not be spared. If those views did not, as is probable, take root in his heart till long afterwards, what interest had Richard to murder an unhappy young prince? This crime therefore was so unnecessary, and is so far from being established by any authority, that he deserves to be entirely acquitted of it.

II. The murder of Henry the Sixth.

This charge, no better supported than the preceding, is still more improbable. "Of the death of this prince, Henry the Sixth," says Fabian, "divers tales wer told. But the most common fame went, that he was sticken with a dagger by the handes of the duke of Gloceter." The author of the Continuation of the Chronicle of Croyland says only, that the body of king Henry was found lifeless (exanime) in the Tower. "Parcat Deus", adds he, "spatium poenitentiae Ei donet, Quicunque sacrilegas manus in Christum Domini ausus est immittere. Unde et agens tyranni, patiensque gloriosi martyris titulum mereatur." The prayer for the murderer, that he may live to repent, proves that the passage was written immediately after the murder was committed. That the assassin deserved the appellation of tyrant, evinces that the historian's suspicions went high; but as he calls him Quicunque, and as we are uncertain whether he wrote before the death of Edward the Fourth or between his death and that of Richard the Third, we cannot ascertain which of the brothers he meant. In strict construction he should mean Edward, because as he is speaking of Henry's death, Richard, then only duke of Gloucester, could not properly be called a tyrant. But as monks were not good grammatical critics, I shall lay no stress on this objection. I do think he alluded to Richard; having treated him severely in the subsequent part of his history, and having a true monkish partiality to Edward, whose cruelty and vices he slightly noticed, in favour to that monarch's severity to heretics and ecclesiastic expiations. "Is princeps, licet diebus suis cupiditatibus & luxui nimis intemperanter indulsisse credatur, in fide tamen catholicus summ, hereticorum severissimus hostis sapientium & doctorum hominum clericorumque promotor amantissimus, sacramentorum ecclesiae devotissimus venerator, peccatorumque fuorum omnium paenitentissimus fuit." That monster Philip the Second possessed just the same virtues. Still, I say, let the monk suspect whom he would, if Henry was found dead, the monk was not likely to know who murdered him—and if he did, he has not told us.

Hall says, "Poore kyng Henry the Sixte, a little before deprived of hys realme and imperial croune, was now in the Tower of London spoyled of his life and all wordly felicite by Richard duke of Gloucester (as the constant fame ranne) which, to the intent that king Edward his brother should be clere out of al secret suspicyon of sudden invasion, murthered the said king with a dagger." Whatever Richard was, it seems he was a most excellent and kind-hearted brother, and scrupled not on any occasion to be the Jack Ketch of the times. We shall see him soon (if the evidence were to be believed) perform the same friendly office for Edward on their brother Clarence. And we must admire that he, whose dagger was so fleshed in murder for the service of another, should be so put to it to find the means of making away with his nephews, whose deaths were considerably more essential to him. But can this accusation be allowed gravely? if Richard aspired to the crown, whose whole conduct during Edward's reign was a scene, as we are told, of plausibility and decorum, would he officiously and unnecessarily have taken on himself the odium of slaying a saint-like monarch, adored by the people? Was it his interest to save Edward's character at the expence of his own? Did Henry stand in his way, deposed, imprisoned, and now childless? The blind and indiscriminate zeal with which every crime committed in that bloody age was placed to Richard's account, makes it greatly probable, that interest of party had more hand than truth in drawing his picture. Other cruelties, which I shall mention, and to which we know his motives, he certainly commanded; nor am I desirous to purge him where I find him guilty: but mob-stories or Lancastrian forgeries ought to be rejected from sober history; nor can they be repeated, without exposing the writer to the imputation of weakness and vulgar credulity.

III. The murder of his brother Clarence.

In the examination of this article, I shall set aside our historians (whose gossipping narratives, as we have seen, deserve little regard) because we have better authority to direct our inquiries: and this is, the attainder of the duke of Clarence, as it is set forth in the Parliamentary History (copied indeed from Habington's Life of Edward the Fourth) and by the editors of that history justly supposed to be taken from Stowe, who had seen the original bill of attainder. The crimes and conspiracy of Clarence are there particularly enumerated, and even his dealing with conjurers and necromancers, a charge however absurd, yet often made use of in that age. Eleanor Cobham, wife of Humphrey duke of Gloucester, had been condemned on a parallel accusation. In France it was a common charge; and I think so late as in the reign of Henry the Eighth Edward duke of Buckingham was said to have consulted astrologers and such like cattle, on the succession of the crown. Whether Clarence was guilty we cannot easily tell; for in those times neither the public nor the prisoner were often favoured with knowing the evidence on which sentence was passed. Nor was much information of that sort given to or asked by parliament itself, previous to bills of attainder. The duke of Clarence appears to have been at once a weak, volatile, injudicious, and ambitious man. He had abandoned his brother Edward, had espoused the daughter of Warwick, the great enemy of their house, and had even been declared successor to Henry the Sixth and his son prince Edward. Conduct so absurd must have left lasting impressions on Edward's mind, not to be effaced by Clarence's subsequent treachery to Henry and Warwick. The Chronicle of Croyland mentions the ill-humour and discontents of Clarence; and all our authors agree, that he kept no terms with the queen and her relations.(1)

Habington adds, that these discontents were secretly fomented by the duke of Gloucester. Perhaps they were: Gloucester certainly kept fair with the queen, and profited largely by the forfeiture of his brother. But where jealousies are secretly fomented in a court, they seldom come to the knowledge of an historian; and though he may have guessed right from collateral circumstances, these insinuations are mere gratis dicta and can only be treated as surmises.(2) Hall, Hollingshed, and Stowe say not a word of Richard being the person who put the sentence in execution; but, on the contrary, they all say he openly resisted the murder of Clarence: all too record another circumstance, which is perfectly ridiculous that Clarence was drowned in a barrel or butt of malmsey. Whoever can believe that a butt of wine was the engine of his death, may believe that Richard helped him into it, and kept him down till he was suffocated. But the strong evidence on which Richard must be acquitted, and indeed even of having contributed to his death, was the testimony of Edward himself. Being some time afterward solicited to pardon a notorious criminal, the king's conscience broke forth; "Unhappy brother!" cried he, "for whom no man would intercede—yet ye all can be intercessors for a villain!" If Richard had been instigator or executioner, it is not likely that the king would have assumed the whole merciless criminality to himself, without bestowing a due share on his brother Gloucester. Is it possible to renew the charge, and not recollect this acquittal?

(1) That chronicle, which now and then, though seldom, is circumstantial, gives a curious account of the marriage of Richard duke of Gloucester and Anne Nevil, which I have found in no other author; and which seems to tax the envy and rapaciousness of Clarence as the causes of the dissention between the brothers. This account, and from a

cotemporary, is the more remarkable, as the Lady Anne is positively said to have been only betrothed to Edward prince of Wales, son of Henry the Sixth, and not his widow, as she is carelessly called by all our historians, and represented in Shakespeare's masterly scene. "Postquam filius regis Henrici, cui Domina Anna, minor filia comitis Warwici, desponsata fuit, in prefato bello de Tewkysbury occubuit," Richard, duke of Gloucester desired her for his wife. Clarence, who had married the elder sister, was unwilling to share so rich an inheritance with his brother, and concealed the young lady. Gloucester was too alert for him, and discovered the Lady Anne in the dress of a cookmaid in London, and removed her to the sanctuary of St. Martin. The brothers pleaded each his cause in person before their elder brother in counsel; and every man, says the author, admired the strength of their respective arguments. The king composed their differences, bestowed the maiden on Gloucester, and parted the estate between him and Clarence; the countess of Warwick, mother of the heiresses, and who had brought that vast wealth to the house of Nevil, remaining the only sufferer, being reduced to a state of absolute necessity, as appears from Dugdale. In such times, under such despotic dispensations, the greatest crimes were only consequences of the economy of government.—Note, that Sir Richard Baker is so absurd as to make Richard espouse the Lady Anne after his accession, though he had a son by her ten years old at that time.

(2) The chronicle above quoted asserts, that the speaker of the house of commons demanded the execution of Clarence. Is it credible that, on a proceeding so public, and so solemn for that age, the brother of the offended monarch and of the royal criminal should have been deputed, or would have stooped to so vile an office? On such occasions

do arbitrary princes want tools? Was Edward's court so virtuous or so humane, that it could furnish no assassin but the first prince of the blood? When the house of commons undertook to colour the king's resentment, was every member of it too scrupulous to lend his hand to the deed?

The three preceding accusations are evidently uncertain and improbable. What follows is more obscure; and it is on the ensuing transactions that I venture to pronounce, that we have little or no authority on which to form positive conclusions. I speak more particularly of the deaths of Edward the Fifth and his brother. It will, I think, appear very problematic whether they were murdered or not: and even if they were murdered, it is impossible to believe the account as fabricated and divulged by Henry the Seventh, on whose testimony the murder must rest at last; for they, who speak most positively, revert to the story which he was pleased to publish eleven years after their supposed deaths, and which is so absurd, so incoherent, and so repugnant to dates and other facts, that as it is no longer necessary to pay court to his majesty, it is no longer necessary not to treat his assertions as an impudent fiction. I come directly to this point, because the intervening articles of the executions of Rivers, Gray, Vaughan, and Hastings will naturally find their place in that disquisition.

And here it will be important to examine those historians on whose relation the story first depends. Previous to this, I must ascertain one or two dates, for they are stubborn evidence and cannot be rejected: they exist every where, and cannot be proscribed even from a Court Calendar.

Edward the Fourth died April 9th, 1483. Edward, his eldest son, was then thirteen years of age. Richard Duke of York, his second son, was about nine.

We have but two contemporary historians, the author of the Chronicle of Croyland, and John Fabian. The first, who wrote in his convent, and only mentioned incidentally affairs of state, is very barren and concise: he appears indeed not to have been ill informed, and sometimes even in a situation of personally knowing the transactions of the times; for in one place we are told in a marginal note, that the doctor of the canon law, and one of the king's councellors, who was sent to Calais, was the author of the Continuation. Whenever therefore his assertions are positive, and not merely flying reports, he ought to be admitted as fair evidence, since we have no better. And yet a monk who busies himself in recording the insignificant events of his own order or monastery, and who was at most occasionally made use of, was not likely to know the most important and most mysterious secrets of state; I mean, as he was not employed in those iniquitous transactions—if he had been, we should learn or might expect still less truth from him.

John Fabian was a merchant, and had been sheriff of London, and died in 1512: he consequently lived on the spot at that very interesting period. Yet no sheriff was ever less qualified to write a history of England. His narrative is dry, uncircumstantial, and unimportant: he mentions the deaths of princes and revolutions of government, with the same phlegm and brevity as he would speak of the appointment of churchwardens. I say not this from any partiality, or to decry the simple man as crossing my opinion; for Fabian's testimony is far from bearing hard against Richard, even though he wrote under Henry the Seventh, who would have suffered no apology for his rival, and whose reign was employed not only in extirpating the house of York, but in forging the most atrocious calumnies to blacken their memories, and invalidate their just claim.

But the great source from whence all later historians have taken their materials for the reign of Richard the Third, is Sir Thomas More. Grafton, the next in order, has copied him verbatim: so does Hollingshed—and we are told by the former in a marginal note, that Sir Thomas was under-sheriff of London when he composed his work. It is in truth a composition, and a very beautiful one. He was then in the vigour of his fancy, and fresh from the study of the Greek and Roman historians, whose manner he has imitated in divers imaginary orations. They serve to lengthen an unknown history of little more than two months into a pretty sizeable volume; but are no more to be received as genuine, than the facts they adduced to countenance. An under-sheriff of London, aged but twenty-eight, and recently marked with the displeasure of the crown, was not likely to be furnished with materials from any high authority, and could not receive them from the best authority, I mean the adverse party, who were proscribed, and all their chiefs banished or put to death. Let us again recur to dates.(3) Sir Thomas More was born in 1480: he was appointed under-sheriff in 1508, and three years before had offended Henry the Seventh in the tender point of opposing a subsidy. Buck, the apologist of Richard the Third, ascribes the authorities of Sir Thomas to the information of archbishop Morton; and it is true that he had been brought up under that prelate; but Morton died in 1500, when Sir Thomas was but twenty years old, and when he had scarce thought of writing history. What materials he had gathered from his master were probably nothing more than a general narrative of the preceding times in discourse at dinner or in a winter's evening, if so raw a youth can be supposed to have been admitted to familiarity with a prelate of that rank and prime minister. But granting that such pregnant parts as More's had leaped the barrier of dignity, and insinuated himself into the archbishop's favour; could he have drawn from a more corrupted source? Morton had not only violated his allegiance to Richard; but had been the chief engine to dethrone him, and to plant a bastard scyon in the throne. Of all men living there could not be more suspicious testimony than the prelate's, except the king's: and had the archbishop selected More for the historian of those dark scenes, who had so much, interest to blacken Richard, as the man who had risen to be prime minister to his rival? Take it therefore either way; that the archbishop did or did not pitch on a young man of twenty to write that history, his authority was as suspicious as could be.

(3) Vide Biog. Britannica, p. 3159.

It may be said, on the other hand, that Sir Thomas, who had smarted for his boldness (for his father, a judge of the king's bench, had been imprisoned and fined for his son's offence) had had little inducement to flatter the Lancastrian cause. It is very true; nor am I inclined to impute adulation to one of the honestest statesmen and brightest names in our annals. He who scorned to save his life by bending to the will of the son, was not likely to canvas the favour of the father, by prostituting his pen to the humour of the court. I take the truth to be, that Sir Thomas wrote his reign of Edward the Fifth as he wrote his Utopia; to amuse his leisure and exercise his fancy. He took up a paltry canvas and embroidered it with a flowing design as his imagination suggested the colours. I should deal more severely with his respected memory on any other hypothesis. He has been guilty of such palpable and material falshoods, as, while they destroy his credit as an historian, would reproach his veracity as a man, if we could impute them to premeditated perversion of truth, and not to youthful levity and inaccuracy. Standing as they do, the sole groundwork of that reign's history, I am authorized to pronounce the work, invention and romance.

Polidore Virgil, a foreigner, and author of a light Latin history, was here during the reigns of Henry the Seventh and Eighth. I may quote him now-and-then, and the Chronicle of Croyland; but neither furnish us with much light.

There was another writer in that age of far greater authority, whose negligent simplicity and' veracity are unquestionable; who had great opportunities of knowing our story, and whose testimony is corroborated by our records: I mean Philip de Comines. He and Buck agree with one another, and with the rolls of parliament; Sir Thomas More with none of them.

Buck, so long exploded as a lover of paradoxes, and as an advocate for a monster, gains new credit the deeper this dark scene is fathomed. Undoubtedly Buck has gone too far; nor are his style or method to be admired. With every intention of vindicating Richard, he does but authenticate his crimes, by searching in other story for parallel instances of what he calls policy.

No doubt politicians will acquit Richard, if confession of his crimes be pleaded in defence of them. Policy will justify his taking off opponents. Policy will maintain him in removing those who would have barred his obtaining the crown, whether he thought he had a right to it, or was determined to obtain it. Morality, especially in the latter case, cannot take his part. I shall speak more to this immediately. Kapin conceived doubts; but instead of pursuing them, wandered after judgments; and they will lead a man where-ever he has a mind to be led. Carte, with more manly shrewdness, has sifted many parts of Richard's story, and guessed happily. My part has less penetration; but the parliamentary history, the comparison of dates, and the authentic monument lately come to light, and from which I shall give extracts, have convinced me, that, if Buck is too favourable, all our other historians are blind guides, and have not made out a twentieth part of their assertions.

The story of Edward the Fifth is thus related by Sir Thomas More, and copied from him by all our historians.

When the king his father died, the prince kept his court at Ludlow, under the tuition of his maternal uncle Anthony earl Rivers. Richard duke of Gloucester was in the north, returning from his successful expedition against the Scots. The queen wrote instantly to her brother to bring up the young king to London, with a train of two thousand horse: a fact allowed by historians, and which, whether a prudent caution or not, was the first overt-act of the new reign; and likely to strike, as it did strike, the duke of Gloucester and the antient nobility with a jealousy, that the queen intended to exclude them from the administration, and to govern in concert with her own family. It is not improper to observe that no precedent authorized her to assume such power. Joan, princess dowager of Wales, and widow of the Black Prince, had no share in the government during the minority of her son Richard the Second. Catherine of Valois, widow of Henry the Fifth Was alike excluded from the regency, though her son was but a year old. And if Isabella governed on the deposition of Edward the Second, it Was by an usurped power, by the same power that had contributed to dethrone her husband; a power sanctified by no title, and confirmed by no act of parliament.(4) The first step to a female regency(5) enacted, though it never took place, was many years afterwards, in the reign of Henry the Eighth.

(4) Twelve guardians were appointed by parliament, and the earl of Lancaster was entrusted with the care of the king's person. The latter, being excluded from exercising his charge by the queen and Mortimer, gave that as a reason for not obeying a summons to parliament. Vide Parliam. Hist. vol. i. p. 208. 215.

(5) Vide the act of succession in Parliam. Hist. vol. III. p. 127.

Edward, on his death-bed, had patched up a reconciliation between his wife's kindred and the great lords of the court; particularly between the Marquis Dorset, the Queen's son, and the lord chamberlain Hastings. Yet whether the disgusted lords had only seemed to yield, to satisfy the dying king, or whether the steps taken by the queen gave them new cause of umbrage it appears that the duke of Buckingham, was the first to communicate his suspicions to Gloucester, and to dedicate himself to his service. Lord Hastings was scarce less forward to join in like measures, and all three, it is pretended, were so alert, that they contrived to have it insinuated to the queen, that it would give much offence if the young king should be brought to London with so great a force as she had ordered; on which suggestions she wrote to Lord Rivers to countermand her first directions.

It is difficult not to suspect, that our historians have imagined more plotting in this transaction than could easily be compassed in so short a period, and in an age when no communication could be carried on but by special messengers, in bad roads, and with no relays of post-horses.

Edward the Fourth died April 9th, and his son made his entrance into London May 4th.(6) It is not probable, that the queen communicated her directions for bringing up her son with an armed force to the lords of the council, and her newly reconciled enemies. But she might be betrayed. Still it required some time for Buckingham to send his servant Percival (though Sir Thomas More vaunts his expedition) to York, where the Duke of Gloucester then lay;(7) for Percival's return (it must be observed too that the Duke of Buckingham was in Wales, consequently did not learn the queen's orders on the spot, but either received the account from London, or learnt it from Ludlow); for the two dukes to send instructions to their confederates in London; for the impression to be made on the queen, and for her dispatching her counter-orders; for Percival to post back and meet Gloucester at Nottingham, and for returning thence and bringing his master Buckingham to meet Richard at Northampton, at the very time of the king's arrival there. All this might happen, undoubtedly; and yet who will believe, that such mysterious and rapid negociations came to the knowledge of Sir Thomas More twenty-five years afterwards, when, as it will appear, he knew nothing of very material and public facts that happened at the same period?

(6) Fabian.

(7) It should be remarked too, that the duke of Gloucester is positively said to be celebrating his brother's obsequies there. It not only strikes off part of the term by allowing the necessary time for the news of king Edward's death to reach York, and for the preparation to be made there to

solemnize a funeral for him; but this very circumstance takes off from the probability of Richard having as yett laid any plan for dispossessing his nephew. Would he have loitered at York at such a crisis, if he had intended to step into the throne?

But whether the circumstances are true, or whether artfully imagined, it is certain that the king, with a small force, arrived at Northampton, and thence proceeded to Stony Stratford. Earl Rivers remained at Northampton, where he was cajoled by the two dukes till the time of rest, when the gates of the inn were suddenly locked, and the earl made prisoner. Early in the morning the two dukes hastened to Stony Stratford, where, in the king's presence, they picked a quarrel with his other half-brother, the lord Richard Grey, accusing him, the marquis Dorset, and their uncle Rivers, of ambitious and hostile designs, to which ends the marquis had entered the Tower, taken treasure thence, and sent a force to sea.

"These things," says Sir Thomas, "the dukes knew, were done for good and necessary purposes, and by appointment of the council; but somewhat they must say," &c. As Sir Thomas has not been pleased to specify those purposes, and as in those times at least privy counsellors were exceedingly complaisant to the ruling powers, he must allow us to doubt whether the purposes of the queen's relations were quite so innocent as he would make us believe; and whether the princes of the blood and the antient nobility had not some reasons to be jealous that the queen was usurping more power than the laws had given her. The catastrophe of her whole family so truly deserves commiseration, that we are apt to shut our eyes to all her weakness and ill-judged policy; and yet at every step we find how much she contributed to draw ruin on their heads and her own, by the confession even of her apologists. The Duke of Gloucester was the first prince of the blood, the constitution pointed him out as regent; no will, no disposition of the late king was even alleged to bar his pretensions; he had served the state with bravery, success, and fidelity; and the queen herself, who had been insulted by Clarence, had had no cause to complain of Gloucester. Yet all her conduct intimated designs of governing by force in the name of her son.(8) If these facts are impartially stated, and grounded on the confession of those who inveigh most bitterly against Richard's memory, let us allow that at least thus far he acted as most princes would have done in his situation, in a lawless and barbarous age, and rather instigated by others, than from any before-conceived ambition and system. If the journeys of Percival are true, Buckingham was the devil that tempted Richard; and if Richard still wanted instigation, then it must follow, that he had not murdered Henry the Sixth, his son, and Clarence, to pave his own way to the crown. If this fine story of Buckingham and Percival is not true, what becomes of Sir Thomas More's credit, on which the whole fabric leans?

Lord Richard, Sir Thomas Vaughan, and Sir Richard Hawte, were arrested, and with Lord Rivers sent prisoners to Pomfret, while the dukes conducted the king by easy stages to London.

The queen, hearing what had happened took sanctuary at Westminster, with her other son the duke of York, and the princesses her daughters. Rotheram, archbishop of York and Lord Chancellor, repaired to her with the great seal, and endeavoured to comfort her dismay with the friendly message he had received from Hastings, who was with the confederate lords on the road. "A woe worth him!" quoth the queen, "for it is he that goeth about to destroy me and my blood!" Not a word is said of her suspecting the duke of Gloucester. The archbishop seems to have been the first who entertained any suspicion; and yet, if all that our historian says of him is true, Rotheram was far from being a shrewd man: witness the indiscreet answer which he is said to have made on this occasion. "Madam," quoth he, "be of good comfort, and assure you, if they crown any other king than your son whom they now have we shall on the morrow crown his brother, whom you have here with you." Did the silly prelate think that it would be much consolation to a mother, whose eldest son might be murthered, that her younger son would be crowned in prison, or was she to be satisfied with seeing one son entitled to the crown, and the other enjoying it nominally?

He then delivered the seal to the queen, and as lightly sent for it back immediately after.

The dukes continued their march, declaring they were bringing the king to his coronation, Hastings, who seems to have preceded them, endeavoured to pacify the apprehensions which had been raised in the people, acquainting them that the arrested lords had been imprisoned for plotting against the dukes of Gloucester and Buckingham. As both those princes were of the blood royal,(9) this accusation was not ill founded, it having evidently been the intention, as I have shewn, to bar them from any share in the administration, to which, by the custom of the realm, they were intitled. So much depends on this foundation, that I shall be excused from enforcing it. The queen's party were the aggressors; and though that alone would not justify all the following excesses, yet we must not judge of those times by the present. Neither the crown nor the great men were restrained by sober established forms and proceedings as they are at present; and from the death of Edward the Third, force alone had dictated. Henry the Fourth had stepped into the throne contrary to all justice. A title so defective had opened a door to attempts as violent; and the various innovations introduced in the latter years of Henry the Sixth had annihilated all ideas of order. Richard duke of York had been declared successor to the crown during the life of Henry and of his son prince Edward, and, as appears by the Parliamentary History, though not noticed by our careless historians was even appointed prince of Wales. The duke of Clarence had received much such another declaration in his favour during the short restoration of Henry. What temptations were these precedents to an affronted prince! We shall see soon what encouragement they gave him to examine closely into his nephew's pretensions; and how imprudent it was in the queen to provoke Gloucester, when her very existence as queen was liable to strong objections. Nor ought the subsequent executions of Lord Rivers, Lord Richard Grey, and of Lord Hastings himself, to be considered in so very strong a light, as they would appear in, if acted in modern times. During the wars of York and Lancaster, no forms of trial had been observed. Not only peers taken in battle had been put to death without process; but whoever, though not in arms, was made prisoner by the victorious party, underwent the same fate; as was the case of Tiptoft earl of Worcester, who had fled and was taken in disguise. Trials had never been used with any degree of strictness, as at present; and though Richard was pursued and killed as an usurper, the Solomon that succeeded him, was not a jot-less a tyrant. Henry the Eighth was still less of a temper to give greater latitude to the laws. In fact, little ceremony or judicial proceeding was observed on trials, till the reign of Elizabeth, who, though decried of late for her despotism, in order to give some shadow of countenance to the tyranny of the Stuarts, was the first of our princes, under whom any gravity or equity was allowed in cases of treason. To judge impartially therefore, we ought to recall the temper and manners of the times we read of. It is shocking to eat our enemies: but it is not so shocking in an Iroquois, as it would be in the king of Prussia. And this is all I contend for, that the crimes of Richard, which he really committed, at least which we have reason to believe he committed, were more the crimes of the age than of the man; and except these executions of Rivers, Grey, and Hastings, I defy any body to prove one other of those charged to his account, from any good authority.

(8) Grafton says, "and in effect every one as he was neerest of kinne unto the queene, so was he planted nere about the prince," p. 761; and again, p. 762, "the duke of Gloucester understanding that the lordes, which were about the king, entended to bring him up to his coronation, accompanied with such power of their friendes, that it should be hard for him, to bring his purpose to passe, without getherying and assemble of people, and in maner of open war," &c. in the same place it appears, that the argument used to dissuade the queen from employing force, was, that it would be a breach of the accommodation made by the late king between her relations and the great lords; and so undoubtedly it was; and though they are accused of violating the peace, it is plain that the queen's insincerity had been at least equal to theirs, and that the infringement of the reconciliation commenced on her side.

(9) Henry duke of Buckingham was the immediate descendant and heir of Thomas of Woodstock duke of Gloucester, the youngest son of Edward the Third, as will appear by this table:

Thomas duke of Gloucester

Anne sole daughter and heiress.

—Edmund earl of Stafford.

Humphrey duke of Bucks.

Humphrey lord Stafford

Henry duke of Bucks.

It is plain, that Buckingham was influenced by this nearness to the crown, for it made him overlook his own alliance with the queen, whose sister he had married. Henry the Eighth did not overlook the proximity of blood, when he afterwards put to death the son of this duke.

It is alleged that the partizans of Gloucester strictly guarded the sanctuary, to prevent farther resort thither; but Sir Thomas confesses too, that divers lords, knights, and gentlemen, either for favour of the queen, or for fear of themselves, Assembled companies and went flocking together in harness. Let us strip this paragraph of its historic buskins, and it is plain that the queen's party took up arms.(10) This is no indifferent circumstance. She had plotted to keep possession of the king, and to govern in his name by force, but had been outwitted, and her family had been imprisoned for the attempt. Conscious that she was discovered, perhaps reasonably alarmed at Gloucester's designs, she had secured herself and her young children in sanctuary. Necessity rather than law justified her proceedings, but what excuse can be made for her faction having recourse to arms? who was authorized, by the tenour of former reigns, to guard the king's person, till parliament should declare a regency, but his uncle and the princes of the blood? endeavouring to establish the queen's authority by force was rebellion against the laws. I state this minutely, because the fact has never been attended to; and later historians pass it over, as if Richard had hurried on the deposition of his nephews without any colour of decency, and without the least provocation to any of his proceedings. Hastings is even said to have warned the citizens that matters were likely to come to a field (to a battle) from the opposition of the adverse party, though as yet no symptom had appeared of designs against the king, whom the two dukes were bringing to his coronation. Nay, it is not probable that Gloucester had as yet meditated more than securing the regency; for had he had designs on the crown, would he have weakened his own claim by assuming the protectorate, which he could not accept but by acknowledging the title of his nephew? This in truth seems to me to have been the case. The ambition of the queen and her family alarmed the princes and the nobility: Gloucester, Buckingham, Hastings, and many more had checked those attempts. The next step was to secure the regency: but none of these acts could be done without grievous provocation to the queen. As soon as her son should come of age, she might regain her power and the means of revenge. Self-security prompted the princes and lords to guard against this reverse, and what was equally dangerous to the queen, the depression of her fortune called forth and revived all the hatred of her enemies. Her marriage had given universal offence to the nobility, and been the source of all the late disturbances and bloodshed. The great earl of Warwick, provoked at the contempt shewn to him by King Edward while negotiating a match for him in France, had abandoned him for Henry the Sixth, whom he had again set on the throne. These calamities were still fresh in every mind, and no doubt contributed to raise Gloucester to the throne, which he could not have attained without almost general concurrence yet if we are to believe historians, he, Buckingham, the mayor of London, and one Dr. Shaw, operated this revolution by a sermon and a speech to the people, though the people would not even give a huzza to the proposal. The change of government in the rehearsal is not effected more easily by the physician and gentleman usher, "Do you take this, and I'll seize t'other chair."

(10) This is confirmed by the chronicle of Croyland, p. 566.

In what manner Richard assumed or was invested with the protectorate does not appear. Sir Thomas More, speaking of him by that title, says "the protector which always you must take for the Duke of Gloucester." Fabian after mentioning the solemn (11) arrival of the king in London, adds, "Than provisyon was made for the kinge's coronation; in which pastime (interval) the duke being admitted for lord protectour." As the parliament was not sitting, this dignity was no doubt conferred on him by the assent of the lords and privy council; and as we hear of no opposition, none was probably made. He was the only person to whom that rank was due; his right could not and does not seem to have been questioned. The Chronicle of Croyland corroborates my opinion, saying, "Accepitque dictus Ricardus dux Glocestriae ilium solennem magistratum, qui duci Humfrido Glocestriae, stante minore aetate regis Henrici, ut regni protector appellaretur, olim contingebat. Ea igitur auctoritate usus est, de consensu & beneplacito omnium dominorum." p. 556.

(11) He was probably eye-witness of that ceremony; for he says, "the king was of the maior and his citizens met at Harnesey parke, the maior and his brethren being clothed in scarlet, and the citizens in violet, to the number of V.C. horses, and than from thence conveyed unto the citie, the king beynge in blewe velvet, and all his lords and servauntes in blacke cloth." p. 513.

Thus far therefore it must be allowed that Richard acted no illegal part, nor discovered more ambition than became him. He had defeated the queen's innovations, and secured her accomplices. To draw off our attention from such regular steps, Sir Thomas More has exhausted all his eloquence and imagination to work up a piteous scene, in which the queen is made to excite our compassion in the highest degree, and is furnished by that able pen with strains of pathetic oratory, which no part of her conduct affords us reason to believe she possessed. This scene is occasioned by the demand of delivering up her second son. Cardinal Bourchier archbishop of Canterbury is the instrument employed by the protector to effect this purpose. The fact is confirmed by Fabian in his rude and brief manner, and by the Chronicle of Croyland, and therefore cannot be disputed. But though the latter author affirms, that force was used to oblige the cardinal to take that step, he by no means agrees with Sir Thomas More in the repugnance of the queen to comply, nor in that idle discussion on the privileges of sanctuaries, on which Sir Thomas has wasted so many words. On the contrary, the chronicle declares, that the queen "Verbis gratanter annues, dimisit puerum." The king, who had been lodged in the palace of the bishop of London, was now removed with his brother to the Tower.

This last circumstance has not a little contributed to raise horror in vulgar minds, who of late years have been accustomed to see no persons of rank lodged in the Tower but state criminals. But in that age the case was widely different. It not only appears by a map engraven so late as the reign of Queen Elizabeth, that the Tower was a royal palace, in which were ranges of buildings called the king's and queen's apartments, now demolished; but it is a known fact, that they did often lodge there, especially previous to their coronations. The queen of Henry the Seventh lay in there: queen Elizabeth went thither after her triumphant entry into the city; and many other instances might be produced, but for brevity I omit them, to come to one of the principal transactions of this dark period: I mean Richard's assumption of the crown. Sir Thomas More's account of this extraordinary event is totally improbable, and positively false in the groundwork of that revolution. He tells us, that Richard meditating usurpation, divided the lords into two separate councils, assembling the king's or queen's party at Baynard's castle, but holding his own private junto at Crosby Place. From the latter he began with spreading murmurs, whispers, and reports against the legality of the late king's marriage. Thus far we may credit him— but what man of common sense can believe, that Richard went so far as publicly to asperse the honor of his own mother? That mother, Cecily duchess dowager of York, a princess of a spotless character, was then living: so were two of her daughters, the duchesses of Suffolk and Burgundy, Richard's own sisters: one of them, the duchess of Suffolk walked at his ensuing coronation, and her son the earl of Lincoln was by Richard himself, after the death of his own son, declared heir apparent to the crown. Is it, can it be credible, that Richard actuated a venal preacher(12) to declare to the people from the pulpit at Paul's cross, that his mother had been an adultress, and that her two eldest sons,(13) Edward the Fourth and the duke of Clarence(14) were spurious; and that the good lady had not given a legitimate child to her husband, but the protector, and I suppose the duchess of Suffolk, though no mention is said to be made of her in the sermon? For as the duchess of Suffolk was older than Richard, and consequently would have been involved in the charge of bastardy, could he have declared her son his heir, he who set aside his brother Edward's children for their illegitimacy? Ladies of the least disputable gallantry generally suffer their husbands to beget his heir; and if doubts arise on the legitimacy of their issue, the younger branches seem most liable to suspicion—but a tale so gross could not have passed even on the mob—no proof, no presumption of the fact was pretended. Were the duchess(15) and her daughters silent on so scandalous an insinuation? Agrippina would scarce have heard it with patience. Moriar modo imperet! said that empress, in her wild wish of crowning her son: but had he, unprovoked, aspersed her honour in the open forum, would the mother have submitted to so unnatural an insult? In Richard's case the imputation was beyond measure atrocious and absurd. What! taint the fame of his mother to pave his way to the crown! Who had heard of her guilt? And if guilty, how came she to stop the career of her intrigues? But Richard had better pretensions, and had no occasion to start doubts even on his own legitimacy, which was too much connected with that of his brothers to be tossed and bandied about before the multitude. Clarence had been solemnly attainted by act of parliament, and his children were out of the question. The doubts on the validity of Edward's marriage were better grounds for Richard's proceedings than aspersion of his mother's honour. On that invalidity he claimed the crown, and obtained it; and with such universal concurrence, that the nation undoubtedly was on his side — but as he could not deprive his nephews, on that foundation, without bastardizing their sisters too, no wonder, the historians, who wrote under the Lancastrian domination, have used all their art and industry to misrepresent the fact. If the marriage of Edward the Fourth with the widow Grey was bigamy, and consequently null, what became of the title of Elizabeth of York, wife of Henry the Seventh? What became of it? Why a bastard branch of Lancaster, matched with a bastard of York, were obtruded on the nation as the right heirs of the crown! and, as far as two negatives can make an affirmative, they were so.

(12) What should we think of a modern historian, who should sink all mention of the convention parliament, and only tell us that one Dr. Burnet got up into the pulpit, and assured the people that Henrietta Maria (a little more suspected of gallantry than duchess Cecily) produced Charles the Second, and James the Second in adultry, and gave no legitimate issue to Charles the First, but Mary princess of Orange, mother of king William; that the people laughed at him, and so the prince of Orange became king?

(13) The Earl of Rutland, another son, elder than Richard, had been murdered at the battle of Wakefield and so was Omitted in that imaginary accusation.

(14) Clarence is the first who is said to have propogated this slandour, and it was much more consonant to his levity and indigested politics, than to the good sense of Richard. We can believe that Richard renewed this story, especially as he must have altered the dates of his mother's amours, and made them continue to her conception of him, as Clarence had made them stop in his own favor?

(15) It appears from Rymer's Foedera, that the very first act of Richard's reign is dated from quadam altera camera juxta capellam in hospitio dominae Ceciliae ducissae Eborum. It does not look much as if he had publicly accused his mother of adultry, when he held his first council at her house. Among the Harleian MSS. in the Museum, No. 2236. art. 6. is the following letter from Richard to this very princess his mother, which is an additional proof of the good terms on which they lived: "Madam, I recomaunde me to you as hertely as is to me possible, beseeching you in my most humble and affectuouse wise of your daly blessing to my synguler comfort and defence in my nede; and, madam, I hertoly beseche you, that I may often here from you to my comfort; and suche newes as be here, my servaunt Thomas Bryan this berer shall showe you, to whom please it you to yeve credence unto. And, madam, I beseche you to be good and graciouse lady to my lord my chamberlayn to be your officer in Wiltshire in suche as Colinbourne had. I trust he shall therein do you good servyce; and that it plese you, that by this barer I may understande your pleasur in this behalve. And I praye God send you th' accomplishement of your noble desires. Written at Pomfret, the thirde day of Juyn, with the hande of your most humble son, Richardus Rex."

Buck, whose integrity will more and more appear, affirms that, before Edward had espoused the lady Grey, he had been contracted to the lady Eleanor Butler, and married to her by the bishop of Bath. Sir Thomas More, on the contrary (and here it is that I am unwillingly obliged to charge that great man with wilful falsehood) pretends that the duchess of York, his mother, endeavouring to dissuade him from so disproportionate an alliance, urged him with a pre-contract to one Elizabeth Lucy, who however, being pressed, confessed herself his concubine; but denied any marriage. Dr. Shaw too, the preacher, we are told by the same authority, pleaded from the pulpit the king's former marriage with Elizabeth Lucy, and the duke of Buckingham is said to have harangued the people to the same effect. But now let us see how the case really stood: Elizabeth Lucy was the daughter of one Wyat of Southampton, a mean gentleman, says Buck, and the wife of one Lucy, as mean a man as Wyat. The mistress of Edward she notoriously was; but what if, in Richard's pursuit of the crown, no question at all was made of this Elizabeth Lucy? We have the best and most undoubted authorities to assure us, that Edward's pre-contract or marriage, urged to invalidate his match with the lady Grey, was with the lady Eleanor Talbot, widow of the lord Butler of Sudeley, and sister of the earl Shrewsbury, one of the greatest peers in the kingdom; her mother was the lady Katherine Stafford, daughter of Humphrey duke of Buckingham, prince of the blood: an alliance in that age never reckoned unsuitable. Hear the evidence. Honest Philip de Comines says(16) "that the bishop of Bath informed Richard, that he had married king Edward to an English lady; and dit cet evesque qu'il les avoit espouses, & que n'y avoit que luy & ceux deux." This is not positive, and yet the description marks out the lady Butler, and not Elizabeth Lucy. But the Chronicle of Croyland is more express. "Color autem introitus & captae possessionis hujusmodi is erat. Ostendebatur per modum supplicationis in quodam rotulo pergameni quod filii Regis Edwardi erant bastardi, supponendo ilium precontraxisse cum quadam domina Alienora Boteler, antequam reginam Elizabeth duxisset uxorem; atque insuper, quod sanguis alterius fratris sui, Georgii ducis Clarentiae, fuisset attinctus; ita quod hodie nullus certus & incorruptus sanguis linealis ex parte Richardi ducis Eboraci poterat inveniri, nisi in persona dicti Richardi ducis Glocestriae. Quo circa supplicabatur ei in fine ejusdem rotuli, ex parte dominorum & communitatis regni, ut jus suum in se assumeret." Is this full? Is this evidence?

(16) Liv. 5, p. 151. In the 6th book, Comines insinuates that the bishop acted out of revenge for having been imprisoned by Edward: it might be so; but as Comines had before alledged that the bishop had actually said he had married them, it might be the truth that the prelate told out of revenge, and not a lie; nor is it probable that his tale would have had any weight, if false, and unsupported by other circumstances.

Here we see the origin of the tale relating to the duchess of York; nullus certus & incorruptus sangnis: from these mistaken or perverted words flowed the report of Richard's aspersing his mother's honour. But as if truth was doomed to emerge, though stifled for near three hundred years, the roll of parliament is at length come to light (with other wonderful discoveries) and sets forth, "that though the three estates which petitioned Richard to assume the crown were not assembled in form of parliament;" yet it rehearses the supplication (recorded by the chronicle above) and declares, "that king Eduard was and stood married and troth plight to one dame Eleanor Butler, daughter to the earl of Shrewsbury, with whom the said king Edward had made a pre-contract of matrimony, long before he made his pretended marriage with Elizabeth Grey." Could Sir Thomas More be ignorant of this fact? or, if ignorant, where is his competence as an historian? And how egregiously absurd is his romance of Richard's assuming the crown inconsequence of Dr. Shaw's sermon and Buckingham's harangue, to neither of which he pretends the people assented! Dr. Shaw no doubt tapped the matter to the people; for Fabian asserts that he durst never shew his face afterwards; and as Henry the Seventh succeeded so soon, and as the slanders against Richard increased, that might happen; but it is evident that the nobility were disposed to call the validity of the queen's marriage in question, and that Richard was solemnly invited by the three estates to accept the regal dignity; and that is farther confirmed by the Chronicle of Croyland, which says, that Richard having brought together a great force from the north, from Wales, and other parts, did on the twenty-sixth of June claim the crown, "seque eodem die apud magnam aulam Westmonasterii in cathedram marmoream ibi intrusit;" but the supplication afore-mentioned had first been presented to him. This will no doubt be called violence and a force laid on the three estates; and yet that appears by no means to have been the case; for Sir Thomas More, partial as he was against Richard, says, "that to be sure of all enemies, he sent for five thousand men out of the north against his coronation, which came up evil apparelled and worse harnessed, in rusty harnesse, neither defensable nor scoured to the sale, which mustured in Finsbury field, to the great disdain of all lookers on." These rusty companions, despised by the citizens, were not likely to intimidate a warlike nobility; and had force been used to extort their assent, Sir Thomas would have been the first to have told us so. But he suppressed an election that appears to have been voluntary, and invented a scene, in which, by his own account, Richard met with nothing but backwardness and silence, that amounted to a refusal. The probability therefore remains, that the nobility met Richard's claim at least half-way, from their hatred and jealousy of the queen's family, and many of them from the conviction of Edward's pre-contract. Many might concur from provocation at the attempts that had been made to disturb the due course of law, and some from apprehension of a minority. This last will appear highly probable from three striking circumstances that I shall mention hereafter.

The great regularity with which the coronation was prepared and conducted, and the extraordinary concourse of the nobility at it, have not all the air of an unwelcome revolution, accomplished merely by violence. On the contrary, it bore great resemblance to a much later event, which, being the last of the kind, we term The Revolution. The three estates of nobility, clergy, and people, which called Richard to the crown, and whose act was confirmed by the subsequent parliament, trod the same steps as the convention did which elected the prince of Orange; both setting aside an illegal pretender, the legitimacy of whose birth was called in question. And though the partizans of the Stuarts may exult at my comparing king William to Richard the Third, it wil be no matter of triumph, since it appears that Richard's cause was as good as King William's, and that in both instances it was a free election. The art used by Sir Thomas More (when he could not deny a pre-contract) in endeavouring to shift that objection on Elizabeth Lucy, a married woman, contrary to the specific words of the act of parliament, betrays the badness of the Lancastrian cause, which would make us doubt or wonder at the consent of the nobility in giving way to the act for bastardizing the children of Edward the Fourth. But reinstate the claim of the lady Butler, which probably was well known, and conceive the interest that her great relations must have made to set aside the queen's marriage, nothing appears more natural than Richard's succession. His usurpation vanishes, and in a few pages more, I shall shew that his consequential cruelty vanishes too, or at most is very, problematic: but first I must revert to some intervening circumstances.

In this whole story nothing is less known to us than the grounds on which lord Hastings was put to death. He had lived in open enmity with the queen and her family, and had been but newly reconciled to her son the marquis Dorset; yet Sir Thomas owns that lord Hastings was one of the first to abet Richard's proceedings against her, and concurred in all the protector's measures. We are amazed therefore to find this lord the first sacrifice under the new government. Sir Thomas More supposes (and he could only suppose; for whatever archbishop Morton might tell him of the plots of Henry of Richmond, Morton was certainly not entrusted with the secrets of Richard) Sir Thomas, I say, supposes, that Hastings either withstood the deposition of Edward the Fifth, or was accused of such a design by Catesby, who was deeply in his confidence; and he owns that the protector undoubtedly loved him well, and loth he was to have him lost. What then is the presumption? Is it not, that Hastings really was plotting to defeat the new settlement contrary to the intention of the three estates? And who can tell whether the suddenness of the execution was not the effect of necessity? The gates of the Tower were shut during that rapid scene; the protector and his adherents appeared in the first rusty armour that was at hand: but this circumstance is alledged against them, as an incident contrived to gain belief, as if they had been in danger of their lives. The argument is gratis dictum: and as Richard loved Hastings and had used his ministry, the probability lies on the other side: and it is more reasonable to believe that Richard acted in self-defence, than that he exercised a wanton, unnecessary, and disgusting cruelty. The collateral circumstances introduced by More do but weaken(17) his account, and take from its probability. I do not mean the silly recapitulation of silly omens which forewarned Hastings of his fate, and as omens generally do, to no manner of purpose; but I speak of the idle accusations put into the mouth of Richard, such as his baring his withered arm, and imputing it to sorcery, and to his blending the queen and Jane Shore in the same plot. Cruel or not, Richard was no fool; and therefore it is highly improbable that he should lay the withering of his arm on recent witchcraft, if it was true, as Sir Thomas More pretends, that it never had been otherwise —but of the blemishes and deformity of his person, I shall have occasion to speak hereafter. For the other accusation of a league between Elizabeth and Jane Shore, Sir Thomas More ridicules it himself, and treats it as highly unlikely. But being unlikely, was it not more natural for him to think, that it never was urged by Richard? And though Sir Thomas again draws aside our attention by the penance of Jane, which she certainly underwent, it is no kind of proof that the protector accused the queen of having plotted(18) with mistress Shore. What relates to that unhappy fair one I shall examine at the end of this work.

Except the proclamation which, Sir Thomas says, appeared to have been prepared before hand. The death of Hastings, I allow, is the fact of which we are most sure, without knowing the immediate motives: we must conclude it was determined on his opposing Richard's claim: farther we do not know, nor whether that opposition was made in a legal or hostile manner. It is impossible to believe that, an hour before his death, he should have exulted in the deaths of their common enemies, and vaunted, as Sir Thomas More asserts, his connection with Richard, if he was then actually at variance with him; nor that Richard should, without provocation, have massacred so excellent an accomplice. This story, therefore, must be left in the dark, as we find it.

(18) So far from it, that as Mr. Hume remarks, there is in Rymer's Foedera a proclamation of Richard, in which he accuses, not the lord Hastings, but the marquis Dorset, of connexion with Jane Shore. Mr. Hume thinks so authentic a paper not sufficient to overbalance the credit due to Sir

Thomas More. What little credit was due to him appears from the course of this work in various and indubitable instances. The proclamation against the lord Dorset and Jane Shore is not dated till the 23rd. of October following. Is it credible that Richard would have made use of this woman's name again, if he had employed it heretofore to blacken Hastings? It is not probable that, immediately on the death of the king, she had been taken into keeping by lord Hastings; but near seven months had elapsed between that death and her connection with the marquis.

The very day on which Hastings was executed, were beheaded earl Rivers, Lord Richard Grey, Vaughan, and Haute. These executions are indubitable; were consonant to the manners and violence of the age; and perhaps justifiable by that wicked code, state necessity. I have never pretended to deny them, because I find them fully authenticated. I have in another(19) place done justice to the virtues and excellent qualities of earl Rivers: let therefore my impartiality be believed, when I reject other facts, for which I can discover no good authority. I can have no interest in Richard's guilt or innocence; but as Henry the Seventh was so much interested to represent him as guilty, I cannot help imputing to the greater usurper, and to the worse tyrant of the two, all that appears to me to have been calumny and misrepresentation.

(19) In the Catalogue of Royal and Noble Authors, vol. 1.

All obstacles thus removed, and Richard being solemnly instated in the throne by the concurrent voice of the three estates, "He openly," says Sir Thomas More, "took upon him to be king the ninth(20) day of June, and' the morrow after was proclaimed, riding to Westminster with great state; and calling the judges before him, straightly commanded them to execute the laws without favor or delay, with many good exhortations, of the which he followed not one." This is an invidious and false accusation. Richard, in his regal capacity, was an excellent king, and for the short time of his reign enacted many wise and wholesome laws. I doubt even whether one of the best proofs of his usurpation was not the goodness of his government, according to a common remark, that princes of doubtful titles make the best masters, as it is more necessary for them to conciliate the favour of the people: the natural corollary from which observation need not be drawn. Certain it is that in many parts of the kingdom not poisoned by faction, he was much beloved; and even after his death the northern counties gave open testimony of their affection to his memory.

(20) Though I have copied our historian, as the rest have copied him, in this date I must desire the reader to take notice, that this very date is another of Sir T. More's errors; for in the public acts is a deed of Edward the Fifth, dated June 17th.

On the 6th of July Richard was crowned, and soon after set out on a progress to York, on his way visiting Gloucester, the seat of his former duchy. And now it is that I must call up the attention of the reader, the capital and bloody scene of Richard's life being dated from this progress. The narrative teems with improbabilities and notorious falshoods, and is flatly contradicted by so many unquestionable facts, that if we have no other reason to believe the murder of Edward the Fifth and his brother, than the account transmitted to us, we shall very much doubt whether they ever were murdered at all. I will state the account, examine it, and produce evidence to confute it, and then the reader will form his own judgment on the matter of fact.

Richard before he left London, had taken no measures to accomplish the assassination; but on the road "his mind misgave him,(21) that while his nephews lived, he should not possess the crown with security. Upon this reflection he dispatched one Richard Greene to Sir Robert Brakenbury, lieutenant of the Tower, with a letter and credence also, that the same Sir Robert in any wise should put the two children to death. This John Greene did his errand to Brakenbury, kneeling before our Lady in the Tower, who plainly answered 'that he never would put them to death, to dye therefore.' Green returned with this answer to the king who was then at Warwick, wherewith he took such displeasure and thought, that the same night he said unto a secret page of his, 'Ah! whom shall a man trust? They that I have brought up myself, they that I thought would have most surely served me, even those faile me, and at my commandment will do nothing for me.' 'Sir,' quoth the page 'there lieth one in the palet chamber without, that I dare say will doe your grace pleasure; the thing were right hard that he would refuse;' meaning this by James Tirrel, whom," says Sir Thomas a few pages afterwards, "as men say, he there made a knight. The man" continues More, "had an high heart, and sore longed upwards, not rising yet so fast as he had hoped, being hindered and kept under by Sir Richard Ratcliffe and Sir William Catesby, who by secret drifts kept him out of all secret trust." To be short, Tirrel voluntarily accepted the commission, received warrant to authorise Brakenbury to deliver to him the keys of the Tower for one night; and having selected two other villains called Miles Forest and John Dighton, the two latter smothered the innocent princes in their beds, and then called Tirrel to be witness of the execution.

(21) Sir T. More.

It is difficult to croud more improbabilities and lies together than are comprehended in this short narrative. Who can believe if Richard meditated the murder, that he took no care to sift Brakenbury before he left London? Who can believe that he would trust so atrocious a commission to a letter? And who can imagine, that on Brakenbury's(22) non-compliance Richard would have ordered him to cede the government of the Tower to Tirrel for one night only, the purpose of which had been so plainly pointed out by the preceding message? And had such weak step been taken, could the murder itself have remained a problem? And yet Sir Thomas More himself is forced to confess at the outset of this very narration, "that the deaths and final fortunes of the two young princes have nevertheless so far come in question, that some remained long in doubt, whether they were in his days destroyed(23) or no." Very memorable words, and sufficient to balance More's own testimony with the most sanguine believers. He adds, "these doubts not only arose from the uncertainty men were in, whether Perkin Warbeck was the true duke of York, but for that also all things were so covertly demeaned, that there was nothing so plain and openly proved, but that yet men had it ever inwardly suspect." Sir Thomas goes on to affirm, "that he does not relate the story after every way that he had heard, but after that way that he had heard it by such men and such meanes as he thought it hard but it should be true." This affirmation rests on the credibility of certain reporters, we do not know whom, but who we shall find were no credible reporters at all: for to proceed to the confutation. James Tirrel, a man in no secret trust with the king, and kept down by Catesby and Ratcliffe, is recommended as a proper person by a nameless page. In the first place Richard was crowned at York (after this transaction) September 8th. Edward the Fourth had not been dead four months, and Richard in possession of any power not above two months, and those very bustling and active: Tirrel must have been impatient indeed, if the page had had time to observe his discontent at the superior confidence of Ratcliffe and Catesby. It happens unluckily too, that great part of the time Ratcliffe was absent, Sir Thomas More himself telling us that Sir Richard Ratcliffe had the custody of the prisoners at Pontefract, and presided at their execution there. But a much more unlucky circumstance is, that James Tirrel, said to be knighted for this horrid service, was not only a knight before, but a great or very considerable officer of the crown; and in that situation had walked at Richard's preceding coronation. Should I be told that Sir Thomas Moore did not mean to confine the ill offices done to Tirrel by Ratcliffe and Catesby solely to the time of Richard's protectorate and regal power, but being all three attached to him when duke of Gloucester, the other two might have lessened Tirrel's credit with the duke even in the preceding reign; then I answer, that Richard's appointing him master of the horse on his accession had removed those disgusts, and left the page no room to represent him as ready through ambition and despondency to lend his ministry to assassination. Nor indeed was the master, of the horse likely to be sent to supercede the constable of the Tower for one night only. That very act was sufficient to point out what Richard desired to, and did, it seems, transact so covertly.

(22) It appears from the Foedera that Brakenbury was appointed Constable of the Tower July 7th; that he surrendered his patent March 9th of the following year, and had one more ample granted to him. If it is supposed that Richard renewed this patent to Sir Robert Brakenbury, to prevent his disclosing what he knew of a murder, in which

he had refused to be concerned, I then ask if it is probable that a man too virtuous or too cautious to embark in an assassination, and of whom the supposed tyrant stood in awe, would have laid down his life in that usurper's cause, as Sir Robert did, being killed on Richard's side at Bosworth, when many other of his adherents betrayed him?

(23) This is confirmed by Lord Bacon: "Neither wanted there even at that time secret rumours and whisperings (which afterwards gathered strength, and turned to great trouble) that the two young sons of king Edward the Fourth, or one of them (which were said to be destroyed in the Tower) were not indeed murthered, but conveyed secretly away, and were yet living." Reign of Henry the Seventh, p. 4. again, p. 19. "And all this time it was still whispered every where that at least one of the children of Edward the Fourth was living."

That Sir James Tirrel was and did walk as master of the horse at Richard's coronation cannot be contested. A most curious, invaluable, and authentic monument has lately been discovered, the coronation-roll of Richard the Third. Two several deliveries of parcels of stuff are there expressly entered, as made to "Sir James Tirrel, knyght, maister of the hors of our sayd soverayn lorde the kynge." What now becomes of Sir Thomas More's informers, and of their narrative, which he thought hard but must be true?

I will go a step farther, and consider the evidence of this murder, as produced by Henry the Seventh some years afterwards, when, instead of lamenting it, it was necessary for his majesty to hope it had been true; at least to hope the people would think so. On the appearance of Perkin Warbeck, who gave himself out for the second of the brothers, who was believed so by most people, and at least feared by the king to be so, he bestirred himself to prove that both the princes had been murdered by his predecessor. There had been but three actors, besides Richard who had commanded the execution, and was dead. These were Sir James Tirrel, Dighton, and Forrest; and these were all the persons whose depositions Henry pretended to produce; at least of two of them, for Forrest it seems had rotted piece-meal away; a kind of death unknown at present to the college. But there were some others, of whom no notice was taken; as the nameless page, Greene, one Black Will or Will Slaughter who guarded the princes, the friar who buried them, and Sir Robert Brakenbury, who could not be quite ignorant of what had happened: the latter was killed at Bosworth, and the friar was dead too. But why was no enquiry made after Greene and the page? Still this silence was not so impudent as the pretended confession of Dighton and Sir James Tyrrel. The former certainly did avow the fact, and was suffered to go unpunished wherever he pleased—undoubtedly that he might spread the tale. And observe these remarkable words of lord Bacon, "John Dighton, who it seemeth spake best the king, was forewith set at liberty." In truth, every step of this pretended discovery, as it stands in lord Bacon, warns us to give no heed to it. Dighton and Tirrel agreed both in a tale, as the king gave out. Their confession therefore was not publickly made, and as Sir James Tirrel was suffered to live;(24) but was shut up in the Tower, and put to death afterwards for we know not what reason. What can we believe, but that Dighton was some low mercenary wretch hired to assume the guilt of a crime he had not committed, and that Sir James Tirrel never did, never would confess what he had not done; and was therefore put out of the way on a fictitious imputation? It must be observed too, that no inquiry was made into the murder on the accession of Henry the Seventh, the natural time for it, when the passions of men were heated, and when the duke of Norfolk, lord Lovel, Catesby, Ratcliffe, and the real abettors or accomplices of Richard, were attainted and executed. No mention of such a murder (25)was made in the very act of parliament that attainted Richard himself, and which would have been the most heinous aggravation of his crimes. And no prosecution of the supposed assassins was even thought of till eleven years afterwards, on the appearance of Perkin Warbeck. Tirrel is not named in the act of attainder to which I have had recourse; and such omissions cannot but induce us to surmise that Henry had never been certain of the deaths of the princes, nor ever interested himself to prove that both were dead, till he had great reason to believe that one of them was alive. Let me add, that if the confessions of Dighton and Tirrel were true, Sir Thomas More had no occasion to recur to the information of his unknown credible informers. If those confessions were not true, his informers were not credible.

(24) It appears by Hall, that Sir James Tirrel had even enjoyed the favor of Henry; for Tirrel is named as captain of Guards in a list of valiant officers that were sent by Henry, in his fifth year, on an expedition into Flanders. Does this look as if Tirrel was so much as suspected of the murder. And who can believe his pretended confession afterwards? Sir James was not executed till Henry's seventeenth year, on suspicion of treason, which suspicion arose on the flight of the earl of Suffolk. Vide Hall's Chronicle, fol. 18 & 55.

(25) There is a heap of general accusations alledged to have been committed by Richard against Henry, in particular of his having shed infant's blood. Was this sufficient specification of the murder of a king? Is it not rather a base way of insinuating a slander, of which no proof could be

given? Was not it consonant to all Henry's policy of involving every thing in obscure and general terms?

Having thus disproved the account of the murder, let us now examine whether we can be sure that the murder was committed.

Of all men it was most incumbent on cardinal Bourchier, archbishop of Canterbury, to ascertain the fact. To him had the queen entrusted her younger son, and the prelate had pledged himself for his security—unless every step of this history is involved in falshood. Yet what was the behaviour of the archbishop? He appears not to have made the least inquiry into the reports of the murder of both children; nay, not even after Richard's death: on the contrary, Bourchier was the very man who placed the crown on the head of the latter;(26) and yet not one historian censures this conduct. Threats and fear could not have dictated this shameless negligence. Every body knows what was the authority of priests in that age; an archbishop was sacred, a cardinal inviolable. As Bourchier survived Richard, was it not incumbant on him to show, that the duke of York had been assassinated in spite of all his endeavours to save him? What can be argued from this inactivity of Bourchier,(27) but that he did not believe the children were murdered.

(26) As cardinal Bourchier set the crown on Richard's head at Westminster, so did archbishop Rotheram at York. These prelates either did not believe Richard had murdered his nephews, or were shamefully complaisant themselves. Yet their characters stand unimpeached in history. Could Richard be guilty, and the archbishops be blameless? Could both be ignorant what was become of the young princes, when both had negotiated with the queen dowager? As neither is accused of being the creature of Richard, it is

probable that neither of them believed he had taken off his nephews. In the Foedera there is a pardon passed to the archbishop, which at first made me suspect that he had taken some part in behalf of the royal children, as he is pardoned for all murders, treasons, concealments, misprisons, riots, routs, &c. but this pardon is not only dated Dec. 13, some months after he had crowned Richard; but, on looking farther, I find such pardons frequently granted to the most eminent of the clergy. In the next reign Walter, archbishop of Dublin, is pardoned all murders, rapes, treasons, felonies, misprisons, riots, routs, extortions, &c.

(27) Lord Bacon tells us, that "on Simon's and Jude's even, the king (Henry the Seventh) dined with Thomas Bourchier, archbishop of Canterburie, and cardinal: and from Lambeth went by land over the bridge to the Tower." Has not this the appearance of some curiosity in the king on the subject of the princes, of whose fate he was uncertain?

Richard's conduct in a parallel case is a strong presumption that this barbarity was falsely laid to his charge. Edward earl of Warwick, his nephew, and son of the duke of Clarence, was in his power too, and no indifferent rival, if king Edward's children were bastards. Clarence had been attainted; but so had almost every prince who had aspired to the crown after Richard the Second. Richard duke of York, the father of Edward the Fourth and Richard the Third, was son of Richard earl of Cambridge, beheaded for treason; yet that duke of York held his father's attainder no bar to his succession. Yet how did Richard the Third treat his nephew and competitor, the young Warwick? John Rous, a zealous Lancastrian and contemporary shall inform us: and will at the same time tell us an important anecdote, maliciously suppressed or ignorantly omitted by all our historians. Richard actually proclaimed him heir to the crown after the death of his own son, and ordered him to be served next to himself and the queen, though he afterwards set him aside, and confined him to the castle of Sheriff-Hutton.(28) The very day after the battle of Bosworth, the usurper Richmond was so far from being led aside from attention to his interest by the glare of his new-acquired crown, that he sent for the earl of Warwick from Sheriff-Hutton and committed him to the Tower, from whence he never stirred more, falling a sacrifice to the inhuman jealousy of Henry, as his sister, the venerable countess of Salisbury, did afterwards to that of Henri the Eight. Richard, on the contrary, was very affectionate to his family: instances appear in his treatment of the earls of Warwick and Lincoln. The lady Ann Poole, sister of the latter, Richard had agreed to marry to the prince of Scotland.

(28) P. 218. Rous is the more to be credited for this fact, as he saw the earl of Warwick in company with Richard at Warwick the year before on the progress to York, which shows that the king treated his nephew with kindness, and did not confine him till the plots of his enemies thickening, Richard found it necessary to secure such as had any pretensions to the crown. This will account for his preferring the earl of Lincoln, who, being his sister's son, could have no prior claim before himself.

The more generous behaviour of Richard to the same young prince (Warwick) ought to be applied to the case of Edward the Fifth, if no proof exists of the murder. But what suspicious words are those of Sir Thomas More, quoted above, and unobserved by all our historians. "Some remained long in doubt," says he, "whether they (the children) were in his (Richard's) days destroyed or no." If they were not destroyed in his days, in whose days were they murdered? Who will tell me that Henry the Seventh did not find, the eldest at least, prisoner in the Tower; and if he did, what was there in Henry's nature or character to prevent our surmizes going farther.

And here let me lament that two of the greatest men in our annals have prostituted their admirable pens, the one to blacken a great prince, the other to varnish a pitiful tyrant. I mean the two (29) chancellors, Sir Thomas More and lord Bacon. The most senseless stories of the mob are converted to history by the former; the latter is still more culpable; he has held up to the admiration of posterity, and what is worse, to the imitation of succeeding princes, a man whose nearest approach to wisdom was mean cunning; and has raised into a legislator, a sanguinary, sordid, and trembling usurper. Henry was a tyrannic husband, and ungrateful master; he cheated as well as oppressed his subjects,(30) bartered the honour of the nation for foreign gold, and cut off every branch of the royal family, to ensure possession to his no title. Had he had any title, he could claim it but from his mother, and her he set aside. But of all titles he preferred that of conquest, which, if allowable in a foreign prince, can never be valid in a native, but ought to make him the execration of his countrymen.

(29) It is unfortunate, that another great chancellor should have written a history with the same propensity to misrepresentation, I mean lord Clarendon. It is hoped no more chancellors will write our story, till they can divest themselves of that habit of their profession, apologizing for a bad cause.

(30) "He had no purpose to go through with any warre upon France; but the truth was, that he did but traffique with that

warre to make his returne in money." Lord Bacon's reign of Henry the Seventh, p. 99.

There is nothing strained in the supposition of Richard's sparing his nephew. At least it is certain now, that though he dispossessed, he undoubtedly treated him at first with indulgence, attention, and respect; and though the proof I am going to give must have mortified the friends of the dethroned young prince, yet it shewed great aversion to cruelty, and was an indication that Richard rather assumed the crown for a season, than as meaning to detain it always from his brother's posterity. It is well known that in the Saxon times nothingwas more common in cases of minority than, for the uncle to be preferred to the nephew; and though bastardizing his brother's children was, on this supposition, double dealing; yet I have no doubt but Richard went so far as to insinuate an intention of restoring the crown when young Edward should be of full age. I have threc strong proofs of this hypothesis. In the first place Sir Thomas More reports that the duke of Buckingham in his conversations with Morton, after his defection from Richard, told the bishop that the protector's first proposal had been to take the crown, till Edward his nephew should attain the age of twenty four years. Morton was certainly competent evidences of these discourses, and therefore a credible one; and the idea is confirmed by the two other proofs I alluded to; the second of which was, that Richard's son did not walk at his father's coronation. Sir Thomas More indeed says that Richard created him prince of Wales on assuming the crown; but this is one of Sir Thomas's misrepresentations, and is contradicted by fact, for Richard did not create his son prince of Wales till he arrived at York; a circumstance that might lead the people to believe that in the interval of the two coronations, the latter of which was celebrated at York, September 8th, the princes were murdered.

But though Richard's son did not walk at his father's coronation, Edward the Fifth probably did, and this is my third proof. I conceive all the astonishment of my readers at this assertion, and yet it is founded on strongly presumptive evidence. In the coronation roll itself(31) is this amazing entry; "To Lord Edward, son of late king Edward the Fourth, for his apparel and array, that is to say, a short gowne made of two yards and three-quarters of crymsy clothe of gold, lyned with two yards of blac velvet, a long gowne made of vi yards of crymsyn cloth of gold lynned with six yards of green damask, a shorte gowne made of two yards of purpell velvett lyned with two yards of green damask, a doublet and a stomacher made of two yards of black satin, &c. besides two foot cloths, a bonnet of purple velvet, nine horse harness, and nine saddle houses (housings) of blue velvet, gilt spurs, with many other rich articles, and magnificent apparel for his henchmen or pages."

(31) This singular curiosity was first mentioned to me by the lord bishop of Carlisle. Mr. Astle lent me an extract of it, with other usual assistances; and Mr. Chamberlain of the great wardrobe obliged me with the perusal of the original; favours which I take this opportunity of gratefully acknowledging.

Let no body tell me that these robes, this magnificence, these trappings for a cavalcade, were for the use of a prisoner. Marvellous as the fact is, there can no longer be any doubt but the deposed young king walked, or it was intended should walk, at his uncle's coronation. This precious monument, a terrible reproach to Sir Thomas More and his copyists, who have been silent on so public an event, exists in the great wardrobe; and is in the highest preservation; it is written on vellum, and is bound with the coronation rolls of Henry the Seventh and Eighth. These are written on paper, and are in worse condition; but that of king Richard is uncommonly fair, accurate, and ample. It is the account of Peter Courteys keeper of the great wardrobe, and dates from the day of king Edward the Fourth his death, to the feast of the purification in the February of the following year. Peter Courteys specifies what stuff he found in the wardrobe, what contracts he made for the ensuing coronation, and the deliveries in consequence. The whole is couched in the most minute and regular manner, and is preferable to a thousand vague and interested histories. The concourse of nobility at that ceremony was extraordinarily great: there were present no fewer than three duchesses of Norfolk. Has this the air of a forced and precipitate election? Or does it not indicate a voluntary concurrence of the nobility? No mention being made in the roll of the young duke of York, no robes being ordered for him, it looks extremely as if he was not in Richard's custody; and strengthens the probability that will appear hereafter, of his having been conveyed away.

There is another article, rather curious than decisive of any point of history. One entry is thus; "To the lady Brygitt, oon of the daughters of K. Edward ivth, being seeke (sick) in the said wardrobe for to have for her use two long pillows of fustian stuffed with downe, and two pillow beres of Holland cloth." The only conjecture that can be formed from this passage is, that the lady Bridget, being lodged in the great wardrobe, was not then in sanctuary.

Can it be doubted now but that Richard meant to have it thought that his assumption of the crown was only temporary? But when he proceeded to bastardize his nephew by act of parliament, then it became necessary to set him entirely aside: stronger proofs of the hastardy might have come out; and it is reasonable to infer this, for on the death of his own son, when Richard had no longer any reason of family to bar his brother Edward's children, instead of again calling them to the succession, as he at first projected or gave out he would, he settled the crown on the issue of his sister, Suffolk, declaring her eldest son the earl of Lincoln his successor. That young prince was slain in the battle of Stoke against Henry the Seventh, and his younger brother the earl of Suffolk, who had fled to Flanders, was extorted from the archduke Philip, who by contrary winds had been driven into England. Henry took a solemn oath not to put him to death; but copying David rather than Solomon he, on his death bed, recommended it to his son Henry the Eighth to execute Suffolk; and Henry the Eighth was too pions not to obey so scriptural an injunction.

Strange as the fact was of Edward the Fifth walking at his successor's coronation, I have found an event exactly parallel which happened some years before. It is well known that the famous Joan of Naples was dethroned and murdered by the man she had chosen for her heir, Charles Durazzo. Ingratitude and cruelty were the characteristics of that wretch. He had been brought up and formed by his uncle Louis king of Hungary, who left only two daughters. Mary the eldest succeeded and was declared king; for that warlike nation, who regarded the sex of a word, more than of a person, would not suffer themselves to be governed by the term queen. Durazzo quitted Naples in pursuit of new ingratitude; dethroned king Mary, and obliged her to walk at his coronation; an insult she and her mother soon revenged by having him assassinated.

I do not doubt but the wickedness of Durazzo will be thought a proper parallel to Richard's. But parallels prove nothing: and a man must be a very poor reasoner who thinks he has an advantage over me, because I dare produce a circumstance that resembles my subject in the case to which it is applied, and leaves my argument just as strong as it was before in every other point.

They who the most firmly believe the murder of the two princes, and from what I have said it is plain that they believe it more strongly than the age did in which it was pretended to be committed; urge the disappearance(32) of the princes as a proof of the murder, but that argument vanishes entirely, at least with regard to one of them, if Perkin Warbeck was the true duke of York, as I shall show that it is greatly probable he was.

(32) Polidore Virgil says, "In vulgas fama valuit filios Edwardi Regis aliquo terrarum partem migrasse, atque ita superstates esse." And the prior of Croyland, not his continuator, whom I shall quote in the next note but one, and who was still better informed, "Vulgatum est Regis Edwardi pueros concessisse in fata, sed quo genere intentus ignoratur."

With regard to the elder, his disappearance is no kind of proof that he was murdered: he might die in the Tower. The queen pleaded to the archbishop of York that both princes were weak and unhealthy. I have insinuated that it is not impossible but Henry the Seventh might find him alive in the Tower.(33) I mention that as a bare possibility—but we may be very sure that if he did find Edward alive there, he would not have notified his existence, to acquit Richard and hazard his own crown. The circumstances of the murder were evidently false, and invented by Henry to discredit Perkin; and the time of the murder is absolutely a fiction, for it appears by the roll of parliament which bastardized Edward the Fifth, that he was then alive, which was seven months after the time assigned by More for his murder, if Richard spared him seven months, what could suggest a reason for his murder afterwards? To take him off then was strengthening the plan of the earl of Richmond, who aimed at the crown by marrying Elizabeth, eldest daughter of Edward the Fourth. As the house of York never rose again, as the reverse of Richard's fortune deprived him of any friend, and as no contemporaries but Fabian and the author of the Chronicle have written a word on that period, and they, too slightly to inform us, it is impossible to know whether Richard ever took any steps to refute the calumny. But we do know that Fabian only mentions the deaths of the princes as reports, which is proof that Richard never declared their deaths, or the death of either, as he would probably have done if he had removed them for his own security. The confessions of Sir Thomas More and lord Bacon that many doubted of the murder, amount to a violent presumption that they were not murdered: and to a proof that their deaths were never declared. No man has ever doubted that Edward the Second, Richard the Second, and Henry the Sixth perished at the times that were given out. Nor Henry the Fourth, nor Edward the Fourth thought it would much help their titles to leave it doubtful whether their competitors existed or not. Observe too, that the chronicle of Croyland, after relating Richard's second coronation at York, says, it was advised by some in the sanctuary at Westminster to convey abroad some of king Edward's daughters, "ut si quid dictis masculis humanitus in Turri contingerat, nihilominus per salvandas personas filiarum, regnum aliquando ad veros rediret haeredes." He says not a word of the princes being murdered, only urges the fears of their friends that it might happen. This was a living witness, very bitter against Richard, who still never accuses him of destroying his nephews, and who speaks of them as living, after the time in which Sir Thomas More, who was not then five years old, declared they were dead. Thus the parliament roll and the chronicle agree, and both contradict More. "Interim & dum haec agerentur (the coronation at York) remanserunt duo predicti Edwardi regis filii sub certa deputata, custodia infra Turrim Londoniarum." These are the express words of the Chronicle, p. 567.

(33) Buck asserts this from the parliament roll. The annotator in Kennett's collection says, "this author would have done much towards the credit he drives at in his history, to have specified the place of the roll and the words thereof, whence such arguments might be gathered: for," adds he, "all histories relate the murders to be committed before this time." I have shown that all histories are reduced to one history, Sir Thomas Moore's; for the rest copy him verbatim; and I have shown that his account is false and improbable. As the roll itself is now printed, in the parliamentary history, vol. 2. I will point out the words that imply Edward the Fifth being alive when the act was passed. "Also it appeareth that all the issue of the said king Edward be bastards and unable to inherit or claim any thing by inheritance, by the law and custom of England." Had Edward the Fifth been dead, would not the act indubitably have run thus, were and be bastards. No, says the act, all the issue are bastards. Who were rendered uncapable to inherit but Edward the Fifth, his brother and sisters? Would not the act have specified the daughters of Edward the Fourth if the sons had been dead? It was to bastardise the

brothers, that the act was calculated and passed; and as the words all the issue comprehend male and females, it is clear that both were intended to be bastardized. I must however, impartially observe that Philip de Comines says, Richard having murdered his nephews, degraded their two sisters in full parliament. I will not dwell on his mistake of mentioning two sisters instead of five; but it must be remarked, that neither brothers or sisters being specified in the act, but under the general term of king Edward's issue, it would naturally strike those who were uncertain what was become of the sons, that this act was levelled against the daughters. And as Comines did not write till some years after the event, he could not help falling into that mistake. For my own part I know not how to believe that Richard would have passed that act, if he had murdered the two princes. It was recalling a shocking crime, and to little purpose; for as no< woman had at that time ever sat on the English throne in her own right, Richard had little reason to apprehend the claim of his nieces.

As Richard gained the crown by the illegitimacy of his nephews, his causing them to be murdered, would not only have shown that he did not trust to that plea, but would have transferred their claim to their sisters. And I must not be told that his intended marriage with his neice is an answer to my argument; for were that imputation true, which is very problematic, it had nothing to do with the murder of her brothers. And here the comparison and irrefragability of dates puts this matter out of all doubt. It was not till the very close of his reign that Richard is even supposed to have thought of marrying his neice. The deaths of his nephews are dated in July or August 1483. His own son did not die till April 1484, nor his queen till March 1485. He certainly therefore did not mean to strengthen his title by marrying his neice to the disinheritance of his own son; and having on the loss of that son, declared his nephew the earl of Lincoln his successor, it is plain that he still trusted to the illegitimacy of his brother's children: and in no case possibly to be put, can it be thought that he wished to give strength to the claim of the princess Elizabeth.

Let us now examine the accusation of his intending to marry that neice: one of the consequences of which intention is a vague suspicion of poisoning his wife. Buck says that the queen was in a languishing condition, and that the physicians declared she could not hold out till April; and he affirms having seen in the earl of Arundel's library a letter written in passionate strains of love for her uncle by Elizabeth to the duke of Norfolk, in which she expressed doubts that the month of April would never arrive. What is there in this account that looks like poison; Does it not prove that Richard would not hasten the death of his queen? The tales of poisoning for a time certain are now exploded; nor is it in nature to believe that the princess could be impatient to marry him, if she knew or thought he had murdered her brothers. Historians tell us that the queen took much to heart the death of her son, and never got over it. Had Richard been eager to ned his niece, and had his character been as impetuously wicked as it is represented, he would not have let the forward princess wait for the slow decay of her rival: nor did he think of it till nine months after the death of his son; which shows it was only to prevent Richmond's marrying her. His declaring his nephew his successor, implies at the same time no thought of getting rid of the queen, though he did not expect more issue from her: and little as Buck's authority is regarded, a contemporary writer confirms the probability of this story. The Chronicle of Croyland says, that at the Christmas festival,(34) men were scandalized at seeing the queen and the lady Elizabeth dressed in robes similar and equally royal. I should suppose that Richard learning the projected marriage of Elizabeth and the earl of Richmond, amused the young princess with the hopes of making her his queen; and that Richard feared that alliance, is plain from his sending her to the castle of Sheriff-Hutton on the landing of Richmond.

(34) "Per haec festa natalia choreis aut tripudiis, variisque mutatoriis vestium Annae reginae atque dominae Elizabeth, primogenitae defuncti regis, eisdem colore & forma distributis nimis intentum est: dictumque a multis est, ipsum regem aut expectata morte reginae aut per divortium, matrimonio cum dicta Elizabeth contrahendo mentem omnibus modis applicare," p. 572. If Richard projected this match at Christmas, he was not likely to let these intentions be perceived so early, nor to wait till March, if he did not know that the queen was incurably ill. The Chronicle says, she died of a languishing distemper. Did that look like poison? It is scarce necessary to say that a dispensation from the pope was in that age held so clear a solution of all obstacles to the marriage of near relations, and was so easily to be obtained or purchased by a great prince, that Richard would not have been thought by his contemporaries to have incurred any guilt, even if he had proposed to wed his neice, which however is far from being clear to have been his intention.

The behaviour of the queen dowager must also be noticed. She was stripped by her son-in-law Henry of all her possessions, and confined to a monastery, for delivering up her daughters to Richard. Historians too are lavish in their censures on her for consenting to bestow her daughter on the murderer of her sons and brother. But if the murder of her sons, is, as we have seen, most uncertain, this solemn charge falls to the ground: and for the deaths of her brothers and lord Richard Grey, one of her elder sons, it has already appeared that she imputed them to Hastings. It is much more likely that Richard convinced her he had not murdered her sons, than that she delivered up her daughters to him believing it. The rigour exercised on her by Henry the Seventh on her countenancing Lambert Simnel, evidently set up to try the temper of the nation in favour of some prince of the house of York, is a violent presumption that the queen dowager believed her second son living: and notwithstanding all the endeavours of Henry to discredit Perkin Warbeck, it will remain highly probable that many more who ought to know the truth, believed so likewise; and that fact I shall examine next.

It was in the second year of Henry the Seventh that Lambert Simnel appeared. This youth first personated Richard duke of York, then Edward earl of Warwick; and was undoubtedly an impostor. Lord Bacon owns that it was whispered every-where, that at least one of the children of Edward the Fourth was living. Such whispers prove two things; one, that the murder was very uncertain: the second, that it would have been very dangerous to disprove the murder; Henry being at least as much interested as Richard had been to have the children dead. Richard had set them aside as bastards, and thence had a title to the crown; but Henry was himself the issue of a bastard line, and had no title at all. Faction had set him on the throne, and his match with the supposed heiress of York induced the nation to wink at the defect in his own blood. The children of Clarence and of the duchess of Suffolk were living; so was the young duke of Buckingham, legitimately sprung from the youngest son of Edward the Third; whereas Henry came of the spurious stock of John of Gaunt, Lambert Simnel appeared before Henry had had time to disgust the nation, as he did afterwards, by his tyranny, cruelty, and exactions. But what was most remarkable, the queen dowager tampered in this plot. Is it to be believed, that mere turbulence and a restless spirit could in a year's time influence that woman to throw the nation again into a civil war, and attempt to dethrone her own daughter? And in favour of whom? Of the issue of Clarence, whom she had contributed to have put to death, or in favour of an impostor? There is not common sense in the supposition. No; she certainly knew or believed that Richard, her second son, had escaped and was living, and was glad to overturn the usurper without risking her child. The plot failed, and the queen dowager was shut up, where she remained till her death, "in prison, poverty, and solitude."(35) The king trumped up a silly accusation of her having delivered her daughters out of sanctuary to King Richard, "which proceeding," says the noble historian, "being even at the time taxed for rigorous and undue, makes it very probable there was some greater matter against her, which the king, upon reason of policie, and to avoid envy, would not publish." How truth sometimes escapes fiom the most courtly pens! What interpretation can be put on these words, but that the king found the queen dowager was privy to the escape at least or existence of her second son, and secured her, lest she should bear testimony to the truth, and foment insurrections in his favour? Lord Bacon adds, "It is likewise no small argument that there was some secret in it; for that the priest Simon himself (who set Lambert to work) after he was taken, was never brought to execution; no, not so much as to publicke triall, but was only shut up close in a dungeon. Adde to this, that after the earl of Lincoln (a principal person of the house of York) was slaine in Stokefield, the king opened himself to some of his councell, that he was sorie for the earl's death, because by him (he said) he might have known the bottom of his danger."

(35) Lord Bacon.

The earl of Lincoln had been declared heir to the crown by Richard, and therefore certainly did not mean to advance Simnel, an impostor, to it. It will be insinuated, and lord Bacon attributes that motive to him, that the earl of Lincoln hoped to open a way to the crown for himself. It might be so; still that will not account for Henry's wish, that the earl had been saved. On the contrary, one dangerous competitor was removed by his death; and therefore when Henry wanted to have learned the bottom of his danger, it is plain he referred to Richard duke of York, of whose fate he was still in doubt.(36) He certainly was; why else was it thought dangerous to visit or see the queen dowager after her imprisonment, as lord Bacon owns it was; "For that act," continucs he, "the king sustained great obliquie; which nevertheless (besides the reason of state) was somewhat sweetened to him In a great confiscation." Excellent prince! This is the man in whose favour Richard the Third is represented as a monster. "For Lambert, the king would not take his life," continues Henry's biographer, "both out of magnanimitie" (a most proper picture of so mean a prince) "and likewise out of wisdom, thinking that if he suffered death he would be forgotten too soon; but being kept alive, he would be a continual spectacle, and a kind of remedy against the like inchantments of people in time to come." What! do lawful princes live in dread of a possibility of phantoms!(37) Oh! no; but Henry knew what he had to fear; and he hoped by keeping up the memory of Simnel's imposture, to discredit the true duke of York, as another puppet, when ever he should really appear.

(36) The earl of Lincoln assuredly did not mean to blacken his uncle Richard by whom he had been declared heir to the crown. One should therefore be glad to know what account he gave of the escape of the young duke of York. Is it probable that the Earl of Lincoln gave out, that the elder had been murdered? It is more reasonable to suppose, that the earl asserted that the child had been conveyed away by means of the queen dowager or some other friend; and before I conclude this examination, that I think will appear most probably to have been the case.

(37) Henry had so great a distrust of his right to the crown in that in his second year he obtained a bull from pope Innocent to qualify the privilege of sanctuaries, in which was this remarkable clause, "That if any took sancturie for case of treason, the king might appoint him keepers to look to him in sanctuarie." Lord Bacon, p. 39.

That appearance did not happen till some years afterwards, and in Henry's eleventh year. Lord Bacon has taken infinite pains to prove a second imposture; and yet owns, "that the king's manner of shewing things by pieces and by darke lights, hath so muffled it, that it hath left it almost a mysterie to this day." What has he left a mystery? and what did he try to muffle? Not the imposture, but the truth. Had so politic a man any interest to leave the matter doubtful? Did he try to leave it so? On the contrary, his diligence to detect the imposture was prodigious. Did he publish his narrative to obscure or elucidate the transaction? Was it his matter to muffle any point that he could clear up, especially when it behoved him to have it cleared? When Lambert Simnel first personated the earl of Warwick, did not Henry exhibit that poor prince one Sunday throughout all the principal streets of London? Was he not conducted to Paul's cross, and openly examined by the nobility? "which did in effect marre the pageant in Ireland." Was not Lambert himself taken into Henry's service, and kept in his court for the same purpose? In short, what did Henry ever muffle and disguise but the truth? and why was his whole conduct so different in the cases of Lambert and Perkin, if their cases were not totally different? No doubt remains in the former; the gross falshoods and contradictions in which Henry's account of the latter is involved, make it evident that he himself could never detect the imposture of the latter, if it was one. Dates, which every historian has neglected, again come to our aid, and cannot be controverted.

Richard duke of York was born in 1474. Perkin Warbeck was not heard of before 1495, when duke Richard would have been Twenty-one. Margaret of York, duchess dowager of Burgundy, and sister of Edward the Fourth, is said by lord Bacon to have been the Juno who persecuted the pious Aeneas, Henry, and set up this phantom against him. She it was, say the historians, and says Lord Bacon, p, 115, "who informed Perkin of all the circumstances and particulars that concerned the person of Richard duke of York, which he was to act, describing unto him the personages, lineaments, and features of the king and queen, his pretended parents, and of his brother and sisters, and divers others that were nearest him in his childhood; together with all passages, some secret, some common that were fit for a child's memory, until the death of king Edward. Then she added the particulars of the time, from the king's death; until he and his brother were committed to the Tower, as well during the time he was abroad, as while he was in sanctuary. As for the times while he was in the Tower, and the manner of his brother's death, and his own escape, she knew they were things that were few could controle: and therefore she taught him only to tell a smooth and likely tale of those matters, warning him not to vary from it." Indeed! Margaret must in truth have been a Juno, a divine power, if she could give all these instructions to purpose. This passage is, so very important, the whole story depends so much upon it, that if I can show the utter impossibility of its being true, Perkin will remain the true duke of York for any thing we can prove to the contrary; and for Henry, Sir Thomas More, lord Bacon, and their copyists, it will be impossible to give any longer credit to their narratives.

I have said that duke Richard was born in 1474. Unfortunately his aunt Margaret was married out of England in 1467, seven years before he was born, and never returned thither. Was not she singularly capable of describing to Perkin, her nephew, whom she had never seen? How well informed was she of the times of his childhood, and of all passages relating to his brother and sisters! Oh! but she had English refugees about her. She must have had many, and those of most intimate connection with the court, if she and they together could compose a tolerable story for Perkin, that was to take in the most minute passages of so many years.(38) Who informed Margaret, that she might inform Perkin, of what passed in sanctuary? Ay; and who told her what passed in the Tower? Let the warmest asserter of the imposture answer that question, and I will give up all I have said in this work; yes, all. Forest was dead, and the supposed priest; Sir James Tirrel, and Dighton, were in Henry's hands. Had they trumpeted about the story of their own guilt and infamy, till Henry, after Perkin's appearance, found it necessary to publish it? Sir James Tirrel and Dighton had certainly never gone to the court of Burgundy to make a merit with Margaret of having murdered her nephews. How came she to know accurately and authentically a tale which no mortal else knew? Did Perkin or did he not correspond in his narrative with Tirrel and Dighton? If he did how was it possible for him to know it? If he did not, is it morally credible that Henry would not have made those variations public? If Edward the Fifth was murdered, and the duke of York saved, Perkin could know it but by being the latter. If he did not know it, what was so obvious as his detection? We must allow Perkin to be the true duke of York, or give up the whole story of Tirrel and Dighton. When Henry had Perkin, Tirrel, and Dighton, in his power, he had nothing to do but to confront them, and the imposture was detected. It would not have been sufficient that Margaret had enjoined him to tell a smooth and likely tale of those matters, A man does not tell a likely tale, nor was a likely tale enough, of matters of which he is totally ignorant.

(38) It would have required half the court of Edward the Fourth to frame a consistent legend Let us state this in a manner that must strike our apprehension. The late princess royal was married out of England, before any of the children of the late prince of Wales were born. She lived no farther than the Hague; and yet who thinks that she could have instructed a Dutch lad in so many passages of the courts of her father and brother, that he would not have been detected in an hour's time. Twenty-seven years at least had elapsed since Margaret had been in the court of England. The marquis of Dorset, the earl of Richmond himself, and most of the fugitives had taken refuge in Bretagne, not with Margaret; and yet was she so informed of every trifling story, even those of the nursery, that she was able to pose Henry himself, and reduce him to invent a tale that had not a shadow of probability in it. Why did he not convict Perkin out of his own mouth? Was it ever pretended that Perkin failed in his part? That was the surest

and best proof of his being an impostor. Could not the whole court, the whole kingdom of England, so cross-examine this Flemish youth, as to catch him in one lie? So; lord Bacon's Juno had inspired him with full knowledge of all that had passed in the last twenty years. If Margaret was Juno, he who shall answer these questions satisfactorily, "erit mihi magnus Apollo."

Still farther: why was Perkin never confronted with the queen dowager, with Henry's own queen, and with the princesses, her sisters? Why were they never asked, is this your son? Is this your brother? Was Henry afraid to trust to their natural emotions?—Yet "he himself," says lord Bacon, p. 186, "saw him sometimes out of a window, or in passage." This implies that the queens and princesses never did see him; and yet they surely were the persons who could best detect the counterfeit, if he had been one. Had the young man made a voluntary, coherent, and credible confession, no other evidence of his imposture would be wanted; but failing that, we cannot help asking, Why the obvious means of detection were not employed? Those means having been omitted, our suspicions remain in full force.

Henry, who thus neglected every means of confounding the impostor, took every step he would have done, if convinced that Perkin was the true duke of York. His utmost industry was exerted in sifting to the bottom of the plot, in learning who was engaged in the conspiracy, and in detaching the chief supporters. It is said, though not affirmatively that to procure confidence to his spies, he caused them to be solemnly cursed at Paul's cross. Certain it is, that, by their information, he came to the knowledge, not of the imposture, but of what rather tended to prove that Perkin was a genuine Plantagenet: I mean, such a list of great men actually in his court and in trust about his person, that no wonder he was seriously alarmed. Sir Robert Clifford,(39) who had fled to Margaret, wrote to England, that he was positive that the claimant was the very identical duke of York, son of Edward the Fourth, whom he had so often seen, and was perfectly acquainted with. This man, Clifford, was bribed back to Henry's service; and what was the consequence? He accused Sir William Stanley, lord Chamberlain, the very man who had set the crown on Henry's head in Bosworth field, and own brother to earl of Derby, the then actual husband of Henry's mother, of being in the conspiracy? This was indeed essential to Henry to know; but what did it proclaim to the nation? What could stagger the allegiance of such trust and such connexions, but the firm persuation that Perkin was the true duke of York? A spirit of faction and disgust has even in later times hurried men into treasonable combinations; but however Sir William Stanley might be dissatisfied, as not thinking himself adequately rewarded, yet is it credible that he should risk such favour, such riches, as lord Bacon allows he possessed, on the wild bottom of a Flemish counterfeit? The lord Fitzwalter and the other great men suffered in the same cause; and which is remarkable, the first was executed at Calais —another presumption that Henry would not venture to have his evidence made public. And the strongest presumption of all is, that not one of the sufferers is pretended to have recanted; they all died then in the persuasion that they had engaged in a righteous cause. When peers, knights of the garter, privy councellors, suffer death, from conviction of a matter of which they were proper judges, (for which of them but must know their late master's son?) it would be rash indeed in us to affirm that they laid down their lives for an imposture, and died with a lie in their mouths.

(39) A gentleman of fame and family, says lord Bacon.

What can be said against king James of Scotland, who bestowed a lady of his own blood in marriage on Perkin? At war with Henry, James would naturally support his rival, whether genuine or suppositious. He and Charles the Eighth both gave him aid and both gave him up, as the wind of their interest shifted about. Recent instances of such conduct have been seen; but what prince has gone so far as to stake his belief in a doubtful cause, by sacrificing a princess of his own blood in confirmation of it?

But it is needless to multiply presumptions. Henry's conduct and the narrative (40) he published, are sufficient to stagger every impartial reader. Lord Bacon confesses the king did himself no good by the publication of that narrative, and that mankind was astonished to find no mention in it of the duchess Margaret's machinations. But how could lord Bacon stop there? Why did he not conjecture that there was no proof of that tale? What interest had Henry to manage a widow of Burgundy? He had applied to the archduke Philip to banish Perkin: Philip replied, he had no power over the lands of the duchess's dowry. It is therefore most credible that the duchess has supported Perkin, on the persuasion he was her nephew; and Henry not being able to prove the reports he had spread of her having trained up an impostor, chose to drop all mention of Margaret, because nothing was so natural as her supporting the heir of her house. On the contrary, in Perkin's confession, as it was called, And which though preserved by Grafton, was suppressed by lord Bacon, not only as repugnant to his lordship's account, but to common sense, Perkin affirms, that "having sailed to Lisbon in a ship with the lady Brampton, who, lord Bacon says, was sent by Margaret to conduct him thither, and from thence have resorted to Ireland, it was at Cork that they of the town first threaped upon him that he was son of the duke of Clarence; and others afterwards, that he was the duke of York." But the contradictions both in lord Bacon's account, and in Henry's narrative, are irreconcileable and unsurmountable: the former solves the likeness,(41) which is allowing the likeness of Perkin to Edward the Fourth, by supposing that the king had an intrigue with his mother, of which he gives this silly relation: that Perkin Warbeck, whose surname it seems was Peter Osbeck, was son of a Flemish converted Jew (of which Hebrew extraction,(42) Perkin says not a word in his confession) who with his wife Katherine de Faro come to London on business; and she producing a son, king Edward, in consideration of the conversion, or intrigue, stood godfather to the child and gave him the name of Peter, Can one help laughing at being told that a king called Edward gave the name of Peter to his godson? But of this transfretation and christening Perkin, in his supposed confession, says not a word, nor pretends to have ever set foot in England, till he landed there in pursuit of the crown; and yet an English birth and some stay, though in his very childhood, was a better way of accounting for the purity of his accent, than either of the preposterous tales produced by lord Bacon or by Henry. The former says, that Perkin, roving up and down between Antwerp and Tournay and other towns, and living much in English company, had the English tongue perfect. Henry was so afraid of not ascertaining a good foundation of Perkin's English accent, that he makes him learn the language twice over.(43) "Being sent with a merchant of Turney, called Berlo, to the mart of Antwerp, the said Berlo set me," says Perkin, "to borde in a skinner's house, that dwelled beside the house of the English nation. And after this the said Berlo set me with a merchant of Middleborough to service for to learne the language,(44) with whom I dwelled from Christmas to Easter, and then, I went into Portugale." One does not learn any language very perfectly and with a good, nay, undistinguishable accent, between Christmas and Easter; but here let us pause. If this account was true, the other relating to the duchess Margaret was false; and then how came Perkin by so accurate a knowledge of the English court, that he did not faulter, nor could be detected in his tale? If the confession was not true, it remains that it was trumped up by Henry, and then Perkin must be allowed the true duke of York.

(40) To what degree arbitrary power dares to trifle with the common sense of mankind has been seen in Portuguese and Russian manifestos.

(41) As this solution of the likeness is not authorized by the youth's supposed narrative, the likeness remains uncontrovertable, and consequently another argument for his being king Edward's son.

(42) On the contrary, Perkins calls his grandfather Diryck Osbeck; Diryck every body knows is Theodoric, and Theodoric is certainly no Jewish appellation. Perkin too mentions several of his relations and their employments at Tournay, without any hint of a Hebrew connection.

(43) Grafton's Chronicle, p 930.

(44) I take this to mean the English language, for these reasons; he had just before named the English nation, and the name of his master was John Strewe, which seems to be an English appellation: but there is a stronger reason for believing it means the English language, which is, that a Flemish lad is not set to learn his own language; though even this absurdity is advanced in this same pretended

confession, Perkin, affirming that his mother, after he had dwelled some time in Tournay, sent him to Antwerp to learn Flemish. If I am told by a very improbable supposition, that French was his native language at Tournay, that he learned Flemish at Antwerp, and Dutch at Middleburg, I will desire the objector to cast his eye on the map, and consider the small distance between Tournay, Middleburg, and Antwerp, and to reflect that the present United Provinces were not then divided from the rest of Flanders; and then to decide whether the dialects spoken at Tournay, Antwerp, and Middleburg were so different in that age, that it was necessary to be set to learn them all separately. If this cannot be answered satisfactorily, it will remain, that Perkin learned Flemish or English twice over. I am indifferent which, for still there will remain a contradiction in the confession. And if English is not meant in the passage above, it will only produce a greater difficulty, which is, that Perkin, at the age of twenty learned to speak English in Ireland with so good an accent, that all England could not discover the cheat. I must be answered too, why lord Bacon rejects the youth's own confession and substitutes another in its place, which makes Perkin born in England, though in his pretended confession Perkin affirms the contrary. Lord Bacon too confirms my interpretation of the passage in question, by saying that Perkin roved up and down between Antwerp and other towns in Flanders, living much in English company, and having the English tongue perfect, p. 115.

But the gross contradiction of all follows: "It was in Ireland," says Perkin, in this very narrative and confession, "that against my will they made me to learne English, and taught me what I should do and say." Amazing! what forced him to learn English, after, as he says himself in the very same page, he had learnt it at Antwerp! What an impudence was there in royal power to dare to obtrude such stuff on the world! Yet this confession, as it is called, was the poor young man forced to read at his execution—no doubt in dread of worse torture. Mr. Hume, though he questions it, owns that it was believed by torture to have been drawn from him. What matters how it was obtained, or whether ever obtained; it could not be true: and as Henry could put together no more plausible account, coommiseration will shed a tear over a hapless youth, sacrificed to the fury and jealousy of an usurper, and in all probability the victim of a tyrant, who has made the world believe that the duke of York, executed by his own orders, had been previously murdered by his predecessor.(45)

(45) Mr. Hume, to whose doubts all respect is due, tells me he thinks no mention being made of Perkin's title in the Cornish rebellion under the lord Audeley, is a strong presumption that the nation was not persuaded of his being the true duke of York. This argument, which at most is negative, seems to me to lose its weight, when it is remembered, that this was an insurrection occasioned by a poll-tax: that the rage of the people was directed against archbishop Morton and Sir Reginald Bray, the supposed authors of the grievance. An insurrection against a tax in a southern county, in which no mention is made of a pretender to the crown, is surely not so forcible a presumption against him, as the persuasion of the northern counties that he was the true heir, is an argument in his favour. Much less can it avail against such powerful evidence as I have shown exists to overturn all that Henry can produce against Perkin.

I have thus, I flatter myself, from the discovery of new authorities, from the comparison of dates, from fair consequences and arguments, and without straining or wresting probability, proved all I pretended to prove; not an hypothesis of Richard's universal innocence, but this assertion with which I set out, that we have no reasons, no authority for believing by far the greater part of the crimes charged on him. I have convicted historians of partiality, absurdities, contradictions, and falshoods; and though I have destroyed their credit, I have ventured to establish no peremptory conclusion of my own. What did really happen in so dark a period, it would be rash to affirm. The coronation and parliament rolls have ascertained a few facts, either totally unknown, or misrepresented by historians. Time may bring other monuments to light(46) but one thing is sure, that should any man hereafter presume to repeat the same improbable tale on no better grounds that it has been hitherto urged, he must shut his eyes against conviction, and prefer ridiculous tradition to the scepticism due to most points of history, and to none more than to that in question.

(46) If diligent search was to be made in the public offices and convents of the Flemish towns in which the duchess Margaret resided, I should not despair of new lights being gained to that part of our history.

I have little more to say, and only on what regards the person of Richard, and the story of Jane Shore; but having run counter to a very valuable modern historian and friend of my own, I must both make some apology for him, and for myself for disagreeing with him.

When Mr. Hume published his reigns of Edward the Fifth, Richard the Third, and Henry the Seventh, the coronation roll had not come to light. The stream of historians concurred to make him take this portion of our story for granted. Buck had been given up as an advancer of paradoxes, and nobody but Carte had dared to controvert the popular belief. Mr. Hume treats Carte's doubts as whimsical: I wonder, he did; he, who having so closely examined our history, had discovered how very fallible many of its authorities are. Mr. Hume himself had ventured to contest both the flattering picture drawn of Edward the First, and those ignominious portraits of Edward the Second, and Richard the Second. He had discovered from Foedera, that Edward the Fourth, while said universally to be prisoner to archbishop Nevil, was at full liberty and doing acts of royal power. Why was it whimsical in Carte to exercise the same spirit of criticism? Mr. Hume could not but know how much the characters of princes are liable to be flattered or misrepresented. It is of little importance to the world, to Mr. Hume, or to me, whether Richard's story is fairly told or not: and in this amicable discussion I have no fear of offending him by disagreeing with him. His abilities and sagacity do not rest on the shortest reign in our annals. I shall therefore attempt to give answers to the questions on which he pins the credibility due to the history of Richard.

The questions are these, 1. Had not the queen-mother and the other heads of the York party been fully assured of the death of both the young princes, would they have agreed to call over the earl of Richmond, the head of the Lancastrian party, and marry him to the princess Elizabeth?—I answer, that when the queen-mother could recall that consent, and send to her son the marquis Dorset to quit Richmond, assuring him of king Richard's favour to him and her house, it is impossible to' say what so weak and ambitious a woman would not do. She wanted to have some one of her children on the throne, in order to recover her own power. She first engaged her daughter to Richmond and then to Richard. She might not know what was become of her sons: and yet that is no proof they were murdered. They were out of her power, whatever was become of them;-and she was impatient to rule. If she was fully assured of their deaths, could Henry, after he came to the crown and had married her daughter, be uncertain of it? I have shown that both Sir Thomas More and lord Bacon own it remained uncertain, and that Henry's account could not be true. As to the heads of the Yorkists;(47) how does it appear they concurred in the projected match? Indeed who were the heads of that party? Margaret, duchess of Burgundy, Elizabeth duchess of Suffolk, and her children; did they ever concur in that match? Did not they to the end endeavour to defeat and overturn it? I hope Mr. Hume will not call bishop Morton, the duke of Buckingham, and Margaret countess of Richmond, chiefs of the Yorkists. 2 The story told constantly by Perkin of his escape is utterly incredible, that those who were sent to murder his brother, took pity on him and granted him his liberty.—Answer. We do not know but from Henry's narrative and the Lancastrian historians that Perkin gave this account.(48) I am not authorized to believe he did, because I find no authority for the murder of the elder brother; and if there was, why is it utterly incredible that the younger should have been spared? 3. What became of him during the course of seven years from his supposed death till his appearance in 1491?—Answer. Does uncertainty of where a man has been, prove his non-identity when he appears again? When Mr. Hume will answer half the questions in this work, I will tell him where Perkin was during those seven years. 4. Why was not the queen-mother, the duchess of Burgundy, and the other friends of the family applied to, during that time, for his support and education?—Answer. Who knows that they were not applied to? The probability is, that they were. The queen's dabbling in the affair of Simnel indicates that she knew her son was alive. And when the duchess of

Burgundy is accused of setting Perkin to work, it is amazing that she should be quoted as knowing nothing about him. 5. Though the duchess of Burgundy at last acknowledged him for her nephew, she had lost all pretence to authority by her former acknowledgment and support of Lambert Simnel, an avowed impostor. — Answer. Mr. Hume here makes an unwary confession by distinguishing between Lambert Simnel, an avowed impostor, and Perkin, whose impostnre was problematic. But if he was a true prince, the duchess could only forfeit credit for herself, not for him: nor would her preparing the way for her nephew, by first playing off and feeling the ground by a counterfeit, be an imputation on her, but rather a proof of her wisdom and tenderness. Impostors are easily detected; as Simnel was. All Henry's art and power could never verify the cheat of Perkin; and if the latter was astonishingly adroit, the king was ridiculously clumsy. 6. Perkin himself confessed his imposture more than once, and read his confession to the people, and renewed his confession at the foot of the gibbet on which he was executed.—Answer. I have shown that this confession was such an aukward forgery that lord Bacon did not dare to quote or adhere to it, but invented a new story, more specious, but equally inconsistent with, probability. 7. After Henry the Eighth's accession, the titles of the houses of York and Lancaster were fully confounded, and there was no longer any necessity for defending Henry the Seventh and his title; yet all the historians of that time, when the events were recent, some of these historians, such as Sir Thomas More, of the highest authority, agree in treating Perkin as an impostor.—Answer. When Sir Thomas More wrote, Henry the Seventh was still alive: that argument therefore falls entirely to the ground: but there was great necessity, I will not say to defend, but even to palliate the titles of both Henry the Seventh and Eighth. The former, all the world agrees now, had no title(49) the latter had none from his father, and a very defective one from his mother, If she had any right, it could only be after her brothers; and it is not to be supposed that so jealous a tyrant as Henry the Eighth would suffer it to be said that his father and mother enjoyed the throne to the prejudice of that mother's surviving brother, in whose blood the father had imbrued his hands. The murder therefore was to be fixed on Richard the Third, who was to be supposed to have usurped the throne, by murdering, and not, as was really the case, by bastardizing his nephews. If they were illegitimate, so was their sister; and if she was, what title had she conveyed to her son Henry the Eighth? No wonder that both Henrys were jealous of the earl of Suffolk, whom one bequeathed to slaughter, and the other executed; for if the children of Edward the Fourth were spurious, and those of Clarence attainted, the right of the house of York was vested in the duchess of Suffolk and her descendants. The massacre of the children of Clarence and the duchess of Suffolk show what Henry the Eighth thought of the titles both of his father and mother.(50) But, says Mr. Hume, all the historians of that time agree in treating Perkin as an impostor. I have shown from their own mouths that they have all doubted of it. The reader must judge between us. But Mr. Hume selects Sir Thomas More as the highest authority; I have proved that he was the lowest—but not in the case of Perkin, for Sir Thomas More's history does not go so low; yet happening to mention him, he says, the man, commonly called Perkin Warbeck, was, as well with the princes as the people, held to be the younger son of Edward the Fourth; and that the deaths of the young' king Edward and of Richard his brother had come so far in question, as some are yet in doubt, whether they were destroyed or no in the days of king Richard. Sir Thomas adhered to the affirmative, relying as I have shown on very bad authorities. But what is a stronger argument ad hominem, I can prove that Mr. Hume did not think Sir Thomas More good authority; no, Mr. Hume was a fairer and more impartial judge: at the very time that he quotes Sir Thomas More, he tacitly rejects his authority; for Mr. Hume, agreeably to truth, specifies the lady Eleanor Butler as the person to whom king Edward was contracted, and not Elizabeth Lucy, as it stands in Sir Thomas More. An attempt to vindicate Richard will perhaps no longer be thought whimsical, when so very acute a reasoner as Mr. Hume could find no better foundation than these seven queries on which to rest his condemnation.

(47) The excessive affection shown by the Northern counties where the principal strength of the Yorkists lay, to Richard the Third while living, and to his memory when dead, implies two things; first, that the party did not give him up to Henry; secondly, that they did not believe he had murdered his nephews, Tyrants of that magnitude are not apt to be popular. Examine the list of the chiefs in Henry's army as stated by the Chronicle of Croyland, p. 574. and they will be found Lancastrians, or very private gentlemen, and but one peer, the earl of Oxford, a noted Lancastrian.

(48) Grafton has preserved a ridiculous oration said to be made by Perkin to the king of Scotland, in which this silly tale is told. Nothing can be depended upon less than such orations, almost always forged by the writer, and unpardonable, if they pass the bounds of truth. Perkin, in the passage in question, uses these words: "And farther to the entent that my life might be in a suretie he (the murderer of my elder brother) appointed one to convey me into some straunge countrie, where, when I was furthest off, and had most neede of comfort, he forsooke me sodainly (I think he was so appointed to do) and left me

desolate alone without friend or knowledge of any relief for refuge," &c. Would not one think one was reading the tale of Valentine and Orson, or a legend of a barbarous age, rather than the History of England, when we are told of strange countries and such indefinite ramblings, as would pass only in a nursery! It remains not only a secret but a doubt, whether the elder brother was murdered. If Perkin was the younger, and knew certainly that his brother was put to death, our doubt would vanish: but can it vanish on no better authority than this foolish oration! Did Grafton hear it pronounced? Did king James bestow his kinswoman on Perkin, on the strength of such a fable?

(49) Henry was so reduced to make out any title to the crown, that he catched even at a quibble. In the act of attainder passed after his accession, he calls himself nephew of Henry the Sixth. He was so, but it was by his father, who was not of the blood royal. Catharine of Valois, after bearing Henry the Sixth, married Owen Tudor, and had two sons, Edmund and Jasper, the former of which married Margaret mother of Henry the Seventh, and so was he half nephew of Henry the Sixth. On one side he had no blood royal, on the other only bastard blood.

(50) Observe, that when Lord Bacon wrote, there was great necessity to vindicate the title even of Henry the Seventh, for James the First claimed from the eldest daughter of Henry and Elizabeth.

With regard to the person of Richard, it appears to have been as much misrepresented as his actions. Philip de Comines, who was very free spoken even on his own masters, and therefore not likely to spare a foreigner, mentions the beauty of Edward the Fourth; but says nothing of the deformity of Richard, though he saw them together.

This is merely negative. The old countess of Desmond, who had danced with Richard, declared he was the handsomest man in the room except his brother Edward, and was very well made. But what shall we say to Dr. Shaw, who in his sermon appealed to the people, whether Richard was not the express image of his father's person, who was neither ugly nor deformed? Not all the protector's power could have kept the muscles of the mob in awe and prevented their laughing at so ridiculous an apostrophe, had Richard been a little, crooked, withered, hump-back'd monster, as later historians would have us believe—and very idly? Cannot a foul soul inhabit a fair body.

The truth I take to have been this. Richard, who was slender and not tall, had one shoulder a little higher than the other: a defect, by the magnifying glasses, of party, by distance of time, and by the amplification of tradition, easily swelled to shocking deformity; for falsehood itself generally pays so much respect to truth as to make it the basis of its superstructures.

I have two reasons for believing Richard was not well made about the shoulders. Among the drawings which I purchased at Vertue's sale was one of Richard and his queen, of which nothing is expressed but the out-lines. There is no intimation from whence the drawing was taken; but by a collateral direction for the colour of the robe, if not copied from a picture, it certainly was from some painted 'window; where existing I do not pretend to say:—in this whole work I have not gone beyond my vouchers. Richard's face is very comely, and corresponds singularly with the portrait of him in the preface to the Royal and Noble Authors. He has a sort of tippet of ermine doubled about his neck, which seems calculated to disguise some want of symmetry thereabouts. I have given two prints(51) of this drawing, which is on large folio paper, that it may lead to a discovery of the original, if not destroyed.

(51) In the prints, the single head is most exactly copied from the drawing, which is unfinished. In the double plate, the reduced likeness of the king could not be so perfectly preserved.

My other authority is John Rous, the antiquary of Warwickshire, who saw Richard at Warwick in the interval of his two coronations, and who describes him thus: "Parvae staturae erat, curtam habens faciem, inaequales humeros, dexter superior, sinisterque inferior." What feature in this portrait gives any idea of a monster? Or who can believe that an eyewitness, and so minute a painter, would have mentioned nothing but the inequality of shoulders, if Richard's form had been a compound of ugliness? Could a Yorkist have drawn a less disgusting representation? And yet Rous was a vehement Lancastrian; and the moment he ceased to have truth before his eyes, gave in to all the virulence and forgeries of his party, telling us in another place, "that Richard remained two years in his mother's womb, and came forth at last with teeth, and hair on his shoulders." I leave it to the learned in the profession to decide whether women can go two years with their burden, and produce a living infant; but that this long pregnancy did not prevent the duchess, his mother, from bearing afterwards, I can prove; and could we recover the register of the births of her children, I should not be surprised to find, that, as she was a very fruitful woman, there was not above a year between the birth of Richard and his preceding brother Thomas.(52) However, an ancient bard,(53) who wrote after Richard was born and during the life of his father, tells us,

Richard liveth yit, but the last of all

Was Ursula, to him whom God list call.

(52) The author I am going to quote, gives us the order in which the duchess Cecily's children were horn thus; Ann duchess of Exeter, Henry, Edward the Fourth Edmund earl of Rutland, Elizabeth duchess of Suffolk, Margaret duchess of Burgundy, William, John, George duke of Clarence, Thomas, Richard the Third, and Ursula. Cox, Im his History of Ireland, says, that Clarence was born in 1451. Buck computed Richard the Third to have fallen at the age of thirty four or five; but, by Cox's account, he could not be more than thirty two. Still this makes it provable, that their mother bore them and their intervening brother Thomas as soon as she well could one after another.

(53) See Vincent's Errors in Brooks's Heraldry, p. 623.

Be it as it will, this foolish tale, with the circumstances of his being born with hair and teeth, was coined to intimate how careful Providence was, when it formed a tyrant, to give due warning of what was to be expected. And yet these portents were far from prognosticating a tyrant; for this plain reason, that all other tyrants have been born without these prognostics. Does it require more time to ripen a foetus, that is, to prove a destroyer, than it takes to form an Aristides? Are there outward and visible signs of a bloody nature? Who was handsomer than Alexander, Augustus, or Louis the Fourteenth? and yet who ever commanded the spilling of more human blood.

Having mentioned John Rous, it is necessary I should say something more of him, as he lived in Richard's time, and even wrote his reign; and yet I have omitted him in the list of contemporary writers. The truth is, he was pointed out to me after the preceding sheets were finished; and upon inspection I found him too despicable and lying an author, even among monkish authors, to venture to quote him, but for two facts; for the one of which as he was an eye-witness, and for the other, as it was of publick notoriety, he is competent authority.

The first is his description of the person of Richard; the second, relating to the young earl of Warwick, I have recorded in its place.

This John Rous, so early as in the reign of Edward the Fourth, had retired to the hermitage of Guy's Cliff, where he was a chantry priest, and where he spent the remaining part of his life in what he called studying and writing antiquities. Amongst other works, most of which are not unfortunately lost, he composed a history of the kings of England. It Begins with the creation, and is compiled indiscriminately from the Bible and from monastic writers. Moses, he tells us, does not mention all the cities founded before the deluge, but Barnard de Breydenback, dean of Mayence, does. With the same taste he acquaints us, that, though the book of Genesis says nothing of the matter, Giraldus Cambrensis writes, that Caphera or Cesara, Noah's niece, being apprehensive of the deluge, set out for Ireland, where, with three men and fifty women, she arrived safe with one ship, the rest perishing in the general destruction.

A history, so happily begun, never falls off: prophecies, omens, judgements, and religious foundations compose the bulk of the book. The lives and actions of our monarchs, and the great events of their reigns, seemed to the author to deserve little place in a history of England. The lives of Henry the Sixth and Edward the Fourth, though the author lived under both, take up but two pages in octavo, and that of Richard the Third, three. We may judge how qualified such an author was to clear up a period so obscure, or what secrets could come to his knowledge at Guy's Cliff: accordingly he retails all the vulgar reports of the times; as that Richard poisoned his wife, and put his nephews to death, though he owns few knew in what manner; but as he lays the scene of their deaths before Richard's assumption of the crown, it is plain he was the worst informed of all. To Richard he ascribes the death of Henry the Sixth; and adds, that many persons believed he executed the murder with his own hands: but he records another circumstance that alone must weaken all suspicion of Richard's guilt in that transaction. Richard not only caused the body to be removed from Chertsey, and solemnly interred at Windsor, but it was publickly exposed, and, if we will believe the monk, was found almost entire, and emitted a gracious perfume, though no care had been taken to embalm it. Is it credible that Richard, if the murderer, would have exhibited this unnecessary mummery, only to revive the memory of his own guilt? Was it not rather intended to recall the cruelty of his brother Edward, whose children he had set aside, and whom by the comparison of this act of piety, he hoped to depreciate(53) in the eyes of the people? The very example had been pointed out to him by Henry the Fifth, who bestowed a pompous funeral on Richard the Second, murdered by order of his father.

(54) This is not a mere random conjecture, but combated by another instance of like address. He deforested a large circuit, which Edward had annexed to the forest of

Whichwoode, to the great annoyance of the subject. This we are told by Rous himself, p. 316,

Indeed the devotion of Rous to that Lancastrian saint, Henry the Sixth, seems chiefly to engross his attention, and yet it draws him into a contradiction; for having said that the murder of Henry the Sixth had made Richard detested by all nations who heard of it, he adds, two pages afterwards, that an embassy arrived at Warwick (while Richard kept his court there) from the king of Spain,(55) to propose a marriage between their children. Of this embassy Rous is a proper witness: Guy's Cliff, I think, is but four miles from Warwick; and he is too circumstancial on what passed there not to have been on the spot. In other respects he seems inclined to be impartial, recording several good and generous acts of Richard.

(55) Drake says, that an ambassador from the queen of Spain was present at Richard's coronation at York. Rous> himself owns, that, amidst a great concourse of nobility that attended the king at York, was the duke of Albany, brother of the king of Scotland. Richard therefore appears not to hav been abhorred by either the courts of Spain or Scotland.

But there is one circumstance, which, besides the weakness and credulity of the man, renders his testimony exceedingly suspicious. After having said, that, if he may speak truth in Richard's favour,(56) he must own that, though small in stature and strength, Richard was a noble knight, and defended himself to the last 'breath with eminent valour, the monk suddenly turns, and apostrophizes Henry the Seventh, to whom be had dedicated his work, and whom he flatters to the best of his poor abilities; but, above all things, for having bestowed the name of Arthur on his eldest son, who, this injudicious and over-hasty prophet forsees, will restore the glory of his great ancestor of the same name. Had Henry christened his second 'son Merlin, I do not doubt but poor Rous would have had still more divine visions about Henry the Eighth, though born to shake half the pillars of credulity.

(56) Attamen si ad ejus honorem veritatem dicam, p. 218.

In short, no reliance can be had on an author of such a frame of mind, so removed from the scene of action, and so devoted to the Welsh intruder on the throne. Superadded to this incapacity and defects, he had prejudices or attachments of a private nature: he had singular affection for the Beauchamps, earls of Warwick, zealous Lancastrians, and had written their lives. One capital crime that he imputes to Richard is the imprisonment of his mother-in-law, Ann Beauchamp countess of Warwick, mother of his queen. It does seem that this great lady was very hardly treated; but I have shown from the Chronicle of Croyland, that it was Edward the Fourth, not Richard, that stripped her of her possessions. She was widow too of that turbulent Warwick the King-maker; and Henry the Seventh bore witness that she was faithfully loyal to Henry the Sixth. Still it seems extraordinary that the queen did not or could not obtain the enlargement of her mother. When Henry the Seventh 'attained the crown, she recovered her liberty 'and vast estates: yet young as his majesty was both in years and avarice, for this munificence took place in his third year, still he gave evidence of the falshood and rapacity of his nature; for though by act of parliament he cancelled the former act that had deprived her, as against all reason, conscience, and course of nature, and contrary to the laws of God and man,(57) and restored her possessions to her, this was but a farce, and like his wonted hypocrisy;

for the very same year he obliged her to convey the whole estate to him, leaving her nothing but the manor of Sutton for her maintenance. Richard had married her daughter; but what claim had Henry to her inheritance? This attachment of Rous to the house of Beauchamp, and the dedication of his work to Henry, Would make his testimony most suspicious, even if he had guarded his work within the rules of probability, and not rendered it a contemptible legend.

(57) Vide Dugdale's Warckshire in Beauchamp.

Every part of Richard's story is involved in obscurity: we neither known what natural children he had, nor what became of them. Stanford says, he had a daughter called Katherine, whom William Herbert earl of Huntingdon covenanted to marry, and to make her a fair and sufficient estate of certain of his manors to the yearly value of 200 pounds over and above all charges. As this lord received a confirmation of his title from Henry the Seventh, no doubt the poor young lady would have been sacrificed to that interest. But Dugdale seems to think she died before the nuptuals were consummated "whether this marriage took effect or not I cannot say; for sure it is that she died in her tender years."(58) Drake(59) affirms, that Richard knighted at York a natural son called Richard of Gloucester, and supposes it to be the same person of whom Peck has preserved so extraordinary an account.(60) But never was a supposition worse grounded. The relation given by the latter of himself, was, that he never saw the king till the night before the battle of Bosworth: and that the king had not then acknowledged, but intended to acknowledge him, if victorious. The deep privacy in which this person had lived, demonstrates how severely the persecution had raged against all that were connected with Richard, and how little truth was to be expected from the writers on the other side. Nor could Peck's Richard Plantagenet be the same person with Richard of Gloucester, for the former was never known till he discovered himself to Sir Thomas More; and Hall says king Richard's natural son was in the hands of Henry the Seventh. Buck says, that Richard made his son Richard of Gloucester, captain of Calais; but it appears from Rymer's Foedera, that Richard's natural son, who was captain of Calais, was called John. None of these accounts accord with Peck's; nor, for want of knowing his mother, can we guess why king Richard was more secret on the birth of this son (if Peck's Richard Plantagenet was truly so) than on those of his other natural children. Perhaps the truest remark that can be made on this whole story is, that the avidity with which our historians swallowed one gross ill-concocted legend, prevented them from desiring or daring to sift a single part of it. If crumbs of truth are mingled with it, at least they are now undistinguishable in such a mass of error and improbability.

(58) Baronage, p. 258.

(58) In his History of York.

(59) See his Desiderata Curiosae.

It is evident from the conduct of Shakespeare, that the house of Tudor retained all their Lancastrian prejudices, even in the reign of queen Elizabeth. In his play of Richard the Third, he seems to deduce the woes of the house of York from the curses which queen Margaret had vented against them; and he could not give that weight to her curses, without supposing a right in her to utter them. This, indeed is the authority which I do not pretend to combat.

Shakespeare's immortal scenes will exist, when such poor arguments as mine are forgotten. Richard at least will be tried and executed on the stage, when his defence remains on some obscure shelf of a library. But while these pages may excite the curiosity of a day, it may not be unentertaining to observe, that there is another of Shakespeare's plays, that may be ranked among the historic, though not one of his numerous critics and commentators have discovered the drift of it; I mean The Winter Evening's Tale, which was certainly intended (in compliment to queen Elizabeth) as an indirect apology for her mother Anne Boleyn. The address of the poet appears no where to more advantage. The subject was too delicate to be exhibited on the stage without a veil; and it was too recent, and touched the queen too nearly, for the bard to have ventured so home an allusion on any other ground than compliment. The unreasonable jealousy of Leontes, and his violent conduct in consequence, form a true portrait of Henry the Eighth, who generally made the law the engine of his boisterous passions. Not only the general plan of the story is most applicable but several passages are so marked, that they touch the real history nearer than the fable. Hermione on her trial says,

. . . . . For honour,

'Tis a derivative from me to mine,

And only that I stand for.

This seems to be taken from the very letter of Anne Boyleyn to the king before her execution, where she pleads for the infant princess his daughter. Mamillius, the young prince, an unnecessary character, dies in his infancy; but it confirms the allusion, as queen Anne, before Elizabeth, bore a still-born son. But the most striking passage,' and which had nothing to do in the Tragedy, but as it pictured Elizabeth, is, where Paulina, describing the new-born princess, and her likeness to her father, says, she has the very trick of his frown. There is one sentence indeed so applicable, both to Elizabeth and her father, that I should suspect the poet inserted it after her death. Paulina, speaking of the child, tells the king,

. . . . . . 'Tis yours;

And might we lay the old proverb to your charge,

So like you, 'tis the worse.

The Winter Evening's Tale was therefore in reality a second part of Henry the Eighth.

With regard to Jane Shore, I have already shown that it was her connection with the marquis Dorset, not with lord Hastings, which drew on her the resentment of Richard. When an event is thus wrested to serve the purpose of a party, we ought to be very cautious how we trust an historian, who is capable of employing truth only as cement in a fabric of fiction. Sir Thomas More tells us, that Richard pretended Jane "was of councell with the lord Hastings to destroy him; and in conclusion, when no colour could fasten upon these matters, then he layd seriously to her charge what she could not deny, namely her adultry; and for this cause, as a godly continent prince, cleane and faultlesse of himself, sent out of heaven into this vicious world for the amendment of mens manners, he caused the bishop of London to put her to open penance."

This sarcasm on Richards morals would have had more weight, if the author had before confined himself to deliver nothing but the precise truth. He does not seem to be more exact in what relates to the penance itself. Richard, by his proclamation, taxed mistress Shore with plotting treason in confederacy with the marquis Dorset. Consequently, it was not from defect of proof of her being accomplice with lord Hastings that she was put to open penance. If Richard had any hand in that sentence, it was, because he had proof of her plotting with the marquis. But I doubt, and with some reason, whether her penance was inflicted by Richard. We have seen that he acknowledged at least two natural children; and Sir Thomas More hints that Richard was far from being remarkable for his chastity. Is it therefore probable, that he acted so silly a farce as to make his brother's mistress do penance? Most of the charges on Richard are so idle, that instead of being an able and artful usurper, as his antagonists allow, he must have been a weaker hypocrite than ever attempted to wrest a sceptre out of the hands of a legal possessor.

It is more likely that the churchmen were the authors of Jane's penance; and that Richard, interested to manage that body, and provoked by her connection with so capital an enemy as Dorset, might give her up, and permit the clergy (who probably had burned incense to her in her prosperity) to revenge his quarrel. My reason for this opinion is grounded on a letter of Richard extant in the Museum, by which it appears that the fair, unfortunate, and aimable Jane (for her virtues far outweighed her frailty) being a prisoner, by Richard's order, in Ludgate, had captivated the king's solicitor, who contracted to marry her. Here follows the letter:

Harl. MSS, No. 2378.

By the KING.

"Right reverend fadre in God, &c. Signifying unto you, that it is shewed unto us, that our servaunt and solicitor, Thomas Lynom, merveillously blinded and abused with the late wife of William Shore, now being in Ludgate by oure commandment, hath made contract of matrymony with hir (as it is said) and entendith, to our full grete merveile, to precede to th' effect of the same. We for many causes wold be sory that hee soo shulde be disposed. Pray you therefore to send for him, and in that ye goodly may, exhorte and sture hym to the contrarye. And if ye finde him utterly set for to marye hur, and noen otherwise will be advertised, then (if it may stand with the lawe of the churche.) We be content (the tyme of marriage deferred to our comyng next to London,) that upon sufficient suerite founde of hure good abering, ye doo send for hure keeper, and discharge him of our said commandment by warrant of these, committing hur to the rule and guiding of hure fadre, or any othre by your discretion in the mene season. Yeven, &c. To the right reverend fadre in God, &c. the bishop of Lincoln, our chauncellour."

It appears from this letter, that Richard thought it indecent for his sollicitor to mary a woman who had suffered public punishment for adultery, and who was confined by his command—but where is the tyrant to be found in this paper? Or, what prince ever spoke of such a scandal, and what is stronger, of such contempt of his authority, with so much lenity and temper? He enjoins his chancellor to dissuade the sollicitor from the match—but should he persist—a tyrant would have ordered the sollicitor to prison too—but Richard —Richard, if his servant will not be dissuaded, allows the match; and in the mean time commits Jane—to whose custody?—Her own father's. I cannot help thinking that some holy person had been her persecutor, and not so patient and gentle a king. And I believe so, because of the salvo for the church: "Let them be married," says Richard, "if it may stand with the lawe of the churche."

From the proposed marriage, one should at first conclude that Shore, the former husband of Jane, was dead; but by the king's query, Whether the marriage would be lawful? and by her being called in the letter the late wife of William Shore, not of the late William Shore, I should suppose that her husband was living, and that the penance itself was the consequence of a suit preferred by him to the ecclesiastic court for divorce. If the injured husband ventured, on the death of Edward the Fourth, to petition to be separated from his wife, it was natural enough for the church to proceed farther, and enjoin her to perform penance, especially when they fell in with the king's resentment to her. Richard's proclamation and the letter above-recited seem to point out this account of Jane's misfortunes; the letter implying, that Richard doubted whether her divorce was so complete as to leave her at liberty to take another husband. As we hear no more of the marriage, and as Jane to her death retained the name of Shore, my solution is corroborated; the chancellor-bishop, no doubt, going more roundly to work than the king had done. Nor, however Sir Thomas More reviles Richard for his cruel usage of mistress Shore, did either of the succeeding kings redress her wrongs, though she lived to the eighteenth year of Henry the Eighth, She had sown her good deeds, her good offices, her alms her charities, in a court. Not one took root;

nor did the ungrateful soil repay her a grain of relief in her penury and comfortless old age.

I have thus gone through the several accusations against Richard; and have shown that they rest on the slightest and most suspicious ground, if they rest on any at all. I have proved that they ought to be reduced to the sole authorities of Sir Thomas More and Henry the Seventh; the latter interested to blacken and misrepresent every action of Richard; and perhaps driven to father on him even his own crimes. I have proved that More's account cannot be true. I have shown that the writers, contemporary with Richard, either do not accuse him, or give their accusations as mere vague and uncertain reports: and what is as strong, the writers next in date, and who wrote the earliest after the events are said to have happened, assert little or nothing from their own information, but adopt the very words of Sir Thomas More, who was absolutely mistaken or misinformed.

For the sake of those who have a mind to canvass this subject, I will recapitulate the most material arguments that tend to disprove what has been asserted; but as I attempt not to affirm what did happen in a period that will still remain very obscure, I flatter myself that I shall not be thought either fantastic or paradoxical, for not blindly adopting an improbable tale, which our historians have never given themselves the trouble to examine.

What mistakes I may have made myself, I shall be willing to acknowledge; what weak reasoning, to give up: but I shall not think that a long chain of arguments, of proofs and probabilities, is confuted at once, because some single fact may be found erroneous. Much less shall I be disposed to take notice of detached or trifling cavils. The work itself is but an inquiry into a short portion of our annals. I shall be content, if I have informed or amused my readers, or thrown any light on so clouded a scene; but I cannot be of opinion that a period thus distant deserves to take up more time than I have already bestowed upon it.

It seems then to me to appear,

That Fabian and the authors of the Chronicle of Croyland, who were contemporaries with Richard, charge him directly with none of the crimes, since imputed to him, and disculpate him of others.

That John Rous, the third contemporary, could know the facts he alledges but by hearsay, confounds the dates of them, dedicated his work to Henry the Seventh, and is an author to whom no credit is due, from the lies and fables with which his work is stuffed.

That we have no authors who lived near the time, but Lancastrian authors, who wrote to flatter Henry the Seventh, or who spread the tales which he invented.

That the murder of prince Edward, son of Henry the Sixth, was committed by king Edward's servants, and is imputed to Richard by no contemporary.

That Henry the Sixth was found dead in the Tower; that it was not known how he came by his death; and that it was against Richard's interest to murder him.

That the duke of Clarence was defended by Richard; that the parliament petitioned for his execution; that no author of the time is so absurd as to charge Richard with being the executioner; and that king Edward took the deed wholly on himself.

That Richard's stay at York on his brother's death had no appearance of a design to make himself king.

That the ambition of the queen, who attempted to usurp the government, contrary to the then established custom of the realm, gave the first provocation to Richard and the princes of the blood to assert their rights; and that Richard was solicited by the duke of Buckingham to vindicate those rights.

That the preparation of an armed force under earl Rivers, the seizure of the Tower and treasure, and the equipment of a fleet, by the marquis Dorset, gave occasion to the princes to imprison the relations of the queen; and that, though they were put to death without trial (the only cruelty which is proved on Richard) it was consonant to the manners of that barbarous and turbulent age, and not till after the queen's party had taken up arms.

That the execution of lord Hastings, who had first engaged with Richard against the queen, and whom Sir Thomas More confesses Richard was lothe to lose, can be accounted for by nothing but absolute necessity, and the law of self-defence.

That Richard's assumption of the protectorate was in every respect agreeable to the laws and usage; was probably bestowed on him by the universal consent of the council and peers, and was a strong indication that he had then no thought of questioning the right of his nephew.

That the tale of Richard aspersing the chastity of his own mother is incredible; it appearing that he lived with her in perfect harmony, and lodged with her in her palace at that very time.

That it is as little credible that Richard gained the crown by a sermon of Dr. Shaw, and a speech of the duke of Buckingham, if the people only laughed at those orators.

That there had been a precontract or marriage between Edward the Fourth and lady Eleanor Talbot; and that Richard's claim to the crown was founded on the illegitimacy of Edward's children.

That a convention of the nobility, clergy, and people invited him to accept the crown on that title.

That the ensuing parliament ratified the act of the convention, and confirmed the bastardy of Edward's children.

That nothing can be more improbable than Richard's having taken no measures before he left London, to have his nephews murdered, if he had any such intention.

That the story of Sir James Tirrel, as related by Sir Thomas More, is a notorious falshood; Sir James Tirrel being at that time master of the horse, in which capacity he had walked at Richard's coronation.

That Tirrel's jealousy of Sir Richard Ratcliffe is another palpable falshood; Tirrel being already preferred, and Ratcliffe absent.

That all that relates to Sir Robert Brackenbury is no less false: Brackenbury either being too good a man to die for a tyrant or murderer, or too bad a man to have refused being his accomplice.

That Sir Thomas More and lord Bacon both confess that many doubted, whether the two princes were murdered in Richard's days or not; and it certainly never was proved that they were murdered by Richard's order.

That Sir Thomas More relied on nameless and uncertain authority; that it appears by dates and facts that his authorities were bad and false; that if Sir James Tirrel and Dighton had really committed the murder and confessed it, and if Perkin Warbeck had made a voluntary, clear, and probable confession of his imposture, there could have remained no doubt of the murder.

That Green, the nameless page, and Will Slaughter, having never been questioned about the murder, there is no reason to believe what is related of them in the supposed tragedy.

That Sir James Tirrel not being attainted on the death of Richard, but having, on the contrary, been employed in great services by Henry the Seventh, it is not probable that he was one of the murderers. That lord Bacon owning that Tirrel's confession did not please the king so well as Dighton's; that Tirrel's imprisonment and execution some years afterwards for a new treason, of which we have no evidence, and which appears to have been mere suspicion, destroy all probability of his guilt in the supposed murder of the children.

That the impunity of Dighton, if really guilty, was scandalous; and can only be accounted for on the supposition of His being a false witness to serve Henry's cause against Perkin Warbeck.

That the silence of the two archbishops, and Henry's not daring to specify the murder of the princes in the act of attainder against Richard, wears all the appearance of their not having been murdered.

That Richard's tenderness and kindness to the earl of Warwick, proceeding so far as to proclaim him his successor, betrays no symptom of that cruel nature, which would not stick at assassinating any competitor.

That it is indubitable that Richard's first idea was to keep the crown but till Edward the Fifth should attain the age of twenty-four.

That with this view he did not create his own son prince of Wales till after he had proved the bastardy of his brother's children.

That there is no proof that those children were murdered.

That Richard made, or intended to make, his nephew Edward the Fifth walk at his coronation.

That there is strong presumption from the parliament-roll and from the Chronicle of Croyland, that both princes were living some time after Sir Thomas More fixes the date of their deaths.

That when his own son was dead, Richard was so far from intending to get rid of his wife that he proclaimed his nephews, first the earl of Warwick, and then the earl of Lincoln, his heirs apparent.

That there is not the least probability of his having poisoned his wife, who died of a languishing distemper: that no proof was ever pretended to be given of it; that a bare supposition of such a crime, without proofs or very strong presumptions, is scarce ever to be credited.

That he seems to have had no intention of marrying his niece, but to have amused her with the hopes of that match, to prevent her marrying Richmond.

That Buck would not have dared to quote her letter as extant in the earl of Arundel's library, if it had not been there: that others of Buck's assertions having been corroborated by subsequent discoveries, leave no doubt of his veracity on this; and that that letter disculpates Richard from poisoning his wife; and only shews the impatience of his niece to be queen.

That it is probable the queen-dowager knew her second son was living, and connived at the appearance of Lambert Simnel, to feel the temper of the nation.

That Henry the Seventh certainly thought that she and the earl of Lincoln were privy to the existence of Richard duke of York, and that Henry lived in terror of his appearance.

That the different conduct of Henry with regard to Lambert Simnel and Perkin Warbeck, implies how different an opinion he had of them; that in the first case, he used natural and most rational methods prove him an impostor; whereas his whole behaviour in Perkin's case was mysterious, and betrayed his belief or doubt that Warbeck was the true duke of York.

That it was morally impossible for the duchess of Burgundy at the distance of twenty-seven years to instruct a Flemish lad so perfectly in all that had passed in the court of England, that he would not have been detected in a few hours.

That she could not inform him, nor could he know, what had passed in the Tower, unless he was the true duke of York.

That if he was not the true duke of York, Henry had nothing to do but to confront him with Tirrel and Dighton, and the imposture must have been discovered.

That Perkin, never being confronted with the queen dowager, and the princesses her daughters, proves that Henry did not dare to trust to their acknowledging him.

That if he was not the true duke of York, he might have been detected by not knowing the queens and princesses, if shown to him without his being told who they were.

That it is not pretended that Perkin ever failed in language, accent,'or circumstances; and that his likeness to Edward the Fourth is allowed.

That there are gross and manifest blunders in his pretended confession.

That Henry was so afraid of not ascertaining a good account of the purity of his English accent, that he makes him learn English twice over.

That lord Bacon did not dare to adhere to this ridiculous account; but forges another, though in reality not much more creditable.

That a number of Henry's best friends, as the lord chamberlain, who placed the crown on his head, knights of the garter, and men of the fairest characters, being persuaded that Perkin was the true duke of York, and dying for that belief, without recanting, makes it very rash to deny that he was so.

That the proclamation in Rymer's Foedera against Jane Shore, for plotting with the marquis Dorset, not with lord Hastings, destroys all the credit of Sir Thomas More, as to what relates to the latter peer.

In short, that Henry's character, as we have received it from his own apologists, is so much worse and more hateful than Richard's, that we may well believe Henry invited and propogated by far the greater part of the slanders against Richard: that Henry, not Richard, probably put to death the true duke of York, as he did the earl of Warwick: and that we are not certain whether Edward the Fifth was murdered; nor, if he was, by whose order he was murdered.

After all that has been said, it is scarcely necessary to add a word on the supposed discovery that was made of the skeletons of the two young princes, in the reign of Charles the Second. Two skeletons found in that dark abyss of so many secret transactions, with no marks to ascertain the time, the age of their interment, can certainly verify nothing. We must believe both princes died there, before we can believe that their bones were found there; and upon what that belief can be founded, or how we shall cease to doubt whether Perkin Warbeck was not one of those children, I am at a loss to guess.

As little is it requisite to argue on the grants made by Richard the Third to his supposed accomplices in that murder, because the argument will serve either way. It was very natural that they, who had tasted most of Richard's bounty, should be suspected as the instruments of his crimes. But till it can be proved that those crimes were committed, it is in vain to bring evidence to show who assisted him in perpetrating them. For my own part, I know not what to think of the death of Edward the Fifth: I can neither entirely acquit Richard of it, nor condemn him; because there are no proofs on either side; and though a court of justice would, from that defect of evidence, absolve him; opinion may fluctuate backward and forwards, and at last remain in suspense.

For the younger brother, the balance seems to incline greatly on the side of Perkin Warbeck, as the true duke of York; and if one was saved, one knows not how nor why to believe that Richard destroyed only the elder.

We must leave this whole story dark, though not near so dark as we found it: and it is perhaps as wise to be uncertain on one portion of our history, as to believe so much as is believed, in all histories, though very probably as falsely delivered to us, as the period which we have here been examining.

ADDITION.

The following notice, obligingly communicated to me by Mr. Stanley, came too late to be inserted in the body of the work, and yet ought not to be omitted.

After the death of Perkin Warbeck, his widow, the lady Catherine Gordon, daughter of the earl of Huntly, from her exquisite beauty, and upon account of her husband called The Rose of Scotland, was married to Sir Matthew Cradock, and is buried with him in Herbert's isle in Swansea church in Wales, where their tomb is still to be seen, with this inscription in ancient characters:

"Here lies Sir Mathie Cradock knight, sume time deputie unto the right honorable Charles Erle of Worcets in the countie of Glamargon. L. Attor. G. R Chauncelor of the same, steward of Gower and Hilrei, and mi ladie, Katerin his wife."

They had a daughter Mary, who was married to Sir Edvard Herbert, son of the first earl of Pembroke, and from that match are descended the earls of Pembroke and countess of Powis, Hans Stanley, Esq, George Rice, Esq. &c.

Printed in Great Britain
by Amazon